God desires you to know and flow in His destiny for your life more than you desire. Now, no more wrong choices and wasted time. Now you will know how to flow into your destiny like a river!

Sid Roth
Host, *It's Supernatural*

D0064194

FLOWING IN
THE RIVER OF
GOD'S
WILL

DESTINY IMAGE BOOKS
BY DENNIS AND JENNIFER CLARK

A Practical Guide to Self-Deliverance

Releasing the Divine Healer Within

The Supernatural Power of Peace

Deep Relief Now: Free, Healed, and Whole

Live Free

Flowing in the River of God's Will

FLOWING IN
THE RIVER OF

GOD'S
WILL

Your Place of
EFFORTLESS TRUST AND PERFECT PEACE

DRS. DENNIS
AND JENNIFER CLARK

DESTINY IMAGE® PUBLISHERS, INC.
P.O. Box 310, Shippensburg, PA 17257-0310
"Promoting Inspired Lives"

This book and all other Destiny Image and Destiny Image Fiction books are available at Christian bookstores and distributors worldwide.

Cover design by Eileen Rockwell
Interior design by Susan Ramundo

For more information on foreign distributors, call 717-532-3040.

Or reach us on the Internet: www.destinyimage.com

ISBN 13 TP: 978-0-7684-1080-8
ISBN 13 EBook: 978-0-7684-1081-5
ISBN 13 HC: 978-0-7684-1835-4
ISBN 13 LP: 978-0-7684-1834-7

For Worldwide Distribution, Printed in the U.S.A.
2 3 4 5 6 / 21 20 19 18

CONTENTS

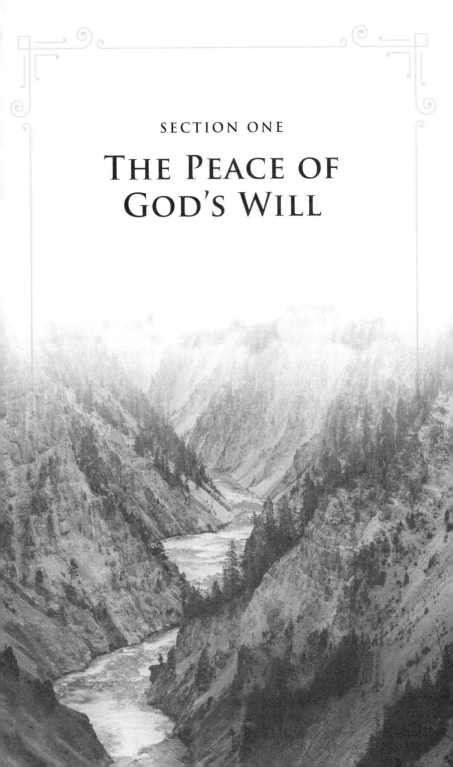

SECTION ONE

THE PEACE OF GOD'S WILL

CHAPTER 1

THE PEACE OF GOD'S WILL

By Jennifer

What if you could tap into a spiritual power source that would make the mighty Niagara Falls look like a trickle? What if you could learn how to function out of that great power to recharge your own life and release healing to the world around you? It would change both you and the world. The truth is…you can.

That power source is in your own heart!

This book is not intended to be a scholarly study of God's will. It is meant to be an encouragement as well as a practical guide so you can learn how to *rest* and enjoy the adventure of life in the river of God's supernatural peace. You see, God's will for us is not a just a plan or a blueprint; it is a heavenly river of supernatural power that gives peace to all who enter its flow.

Jesus promised us access to a continuously flowing artesian well of living waters in our heart—the river of peace. When we live in the peace of God, we tap into the ever-flowing river of God's will that leads to destiny.

LET PEACE RULE

Prior to leaving on a ministry trip to New England many years ago, the Lord took us through a series of lessons about the rule of peace (see Colossians 3:15). When God uses object lessons to teach us, we never forget!

The drive back from the meeting in West Haven, Connecticut, was a breeze—at first. Our hotel was only one hour away, and we expected to be "home" around ten o'clock in the evening. Even when we headed north on I-95, traffic was sparse. That was a pleasant surprise. I-95 is often backed up with rush hour congestion, road construction, or accidents. The traffic was even lighter as we pulled onto I-91 north. It had been a great day ending in an easy drive back to the hotel where we were staying.

On the last mile of our journey, we pulled off the exit ramp onto I-84. Our hotel was directly off the very next exit. However, our eyes widened in shocked dismay when we saw what lay directly before us. There was no turning back, so we reluctantly pulled onto the interstate and were slowly drawn into a vast "parking lot" of cars. We were trapped. No one could move. Some vehicles were even attempting to turn around and go down the exit ramps.

A few car lengths ahead, we saw a policeman running crime scene tape all the way across the highway, from the edge of the road to the concrete barrier median wall. Other police officers walked among the cars picking up items and dropping them in evidence bags. We found out later that we had driven right into the aftermath of a shootout between two cars that started in Hartford and had continued as they sped eastward. The highway had become a crime scene!

Now what? We looked at one another and agreed this was a perfect time to practice peace. After Dennis and I were married in 1997, I asked him to disciple me in all the lessons God had taught him about living in the Spirit. One of the most important lessons of all was the power of peace.

Immediately before leaving on this trip, we had made a conscious decision to let the peace of God rule in our hearts no matter what happened. Because the Bible tells us to let peace rule, obviously God has given us the capacity to do just that: *"Let the peace of God rule in your hearts"* (Colossians 3:15). Therefore, we immediately released our worries and yielded to the presence of God in our hearts. As we did so, the peace of God flooded the car.

Let peace rule no matter what!

We didn't have any idea what would transpire, but we had an inner assurance that God was with us because we could feel His peace. Would we be stuck in this traffic jam for hours? Was there any way out of this? We didn't know the answers, but had a strong assurance that the One who is the Answer was with us. We just didn't know if it was God's will for us to stay there for hours or for traffic to start moving again. Regardless of the outcome, we were determined to stay at peace.

Suddenly, Dennis noticed an opening of about one car length one lane over, right beside the concrete wall. He felt a quickening in his spirit, so without questioning, Dennis immediately pulled into the space. In the natural, it seemed foolish. After all, everyone else was trying to get closer to the side of the road in hope of escaping down a ramp. Much to our amazement, as soon as we pulled into the space, a police officer walked to the wall, peeled back the yellow tape and opened a way for one lane to move forward. About eight cars pulled forward onto the empty interstate ahead and into freedom. We were the last car through. As soon as we passed, the policeman put the tape back in place. To this day, we believe God sent an angel to rescue us.

We were at our hotel five minutes later. The following day we discovered that traffic was at a complete standstill on I-84 until six o'clock the next morning!

On this same trip, we encountered one difficult situation after another. The computer crashed. Our car window was smashed in a robbery and our GPS stolen. The hotel room flooded. Each time we stayed in peace, we saw God move in marvelous ways. In situations that look dire to us, God delights in working on our behalf… when we maintain the right attitude.

Peace is evidence our heart is aligned with the *will of God*. When we have peace, we are connected with God's Kingdom and His purposes. Every time we trust in God and don't give in to fear, we stay in peace. A heart at peace *positions us* so God can move on our behalf. When our heart draws near to God, we feel His peace. When we are at peace, we know God is with us (see James 4:8).

*[W]e know that all things work together for good to those who love God, to those who are the called according to **His purpose*** (Romans 8:28).

GIFT OF PEACE

Dennis had taught me all about abiding in the peace of God as a lifestyle and encouraged me to practice maintaining my peace no matter what happened in everyday life. This was certainly a new concept for me; because I had lived in almost constant anxiety for most of my adult life. When we were first married, Dennis called me "little much afraid" after a character in Hannah Hurnard's *Hinds Feet on High Places*. During the first couple of months of our marriage, Dennis prayed me through the baggage of the past and taught me how to take all fearful thoughts "captive" by releasing them to Christ in my heart.

…Christ in you, the hope of glory (Colossians 1:27).

Jesus Himself said He has given us access to the riches of His Kingdom in our own heart. *"The kingdom of God is within you"* (Luke 17:21). Therefore, when Jesus says He has given us His peace as a gift, it stands to reason that He never takes it away from us.

However, we can lose our *awareness* of the peace of   ***Jesus Himself is***
His presence when carnal emotions of fear, anger,   ***our peace.***
or pain take over.

He Himself is our peace, so His peace is evidence He is with
us (see Ephesians 2:15).

> *Peace I leave with you, My peace I give to you; not as the*
> *world gives do I give to you...* (John 14:27).

FRUIT OF PEACE

Prior to meeting Dennis, I had understood intellectually that
peace is a fruit of the Spirit, but this seemed like a poetic concept
rather than something to actually experience (Galatians 5:22-23).
However, I now learned that supernatural peace is also *tangible
evidence* that the Kingdom of God is with us.

No one had ever shown me how to tap into the fruit of the
Spirit before. Based on what I had observed in church over the
years, I strongly suspected that living in peace was   ***Spiritual reality***
a mystery for most believers. One of the first times   ***is a matter of***
Dennis prayed with me, he instructed me to close   ***the heart.***
my eyes and focus on Christ within. I noticed
that prayer felt different from my customary tension and anxiety
(see Philippians 4:6). When I worried, I felt fear. In prayer, I felt...
peaceful! Dennis explained that I perceived supernatural peace because I was drawing close to God in my heart. You see, the Lord
never leaves us but *our heart* can depart from Him (see Matthew
15:8).

POWER OF PEACE

What does "peace" mean to you? Before I met Dennis, I
thought of peace as tranquility or an absence of discord. Peace as
power was a strange concept for me at first. Dennis told me about

an incident that occurred when he was a new believer that shattered that paradigm instantly.

Soon after he was saved, Dennis volunteered to work at a Christian halfway house for convicts who were out of prison but not quite ready to be assimilated back into society. Needless to say, they were rough characters. Dennis had noticed that he and others could sense the change in the atmosphere of the house when one of the inmates was about to make a break for it or do something violent.

On one particular day, an ominous feeling was particularly strong in the atmosphere. Suddenly one of the men raced into the kitchen, grabbed a butcher knife off the counter, and headed straight for the exit. Dennis was standing directly in front of the only door of escape. Much to his amazement, he felt peace increase so much it seemed to fill him inside and surround him like external armor.

Under ordinary circumstances, Dennis says he would have moved out of the way. That was the sensible thing to do. However, he got the strong impression to hold his ground due to the sheer power of this supernatural peace. The man snarled, "Get out of my way or I'll cut you to pieces!" Dennis stood still. Suddenly, the convict's hand started to tremble. Then he dropped the knife, fell to his knees, and started to cry.

Peace is powerful!

Once when Jesus and His disciples were on the Sea of Galilee in a fishing boat, a sudden and fierce storm arose that seemed to threaten their very lives (see Mark 4:36-40). As *Peace is powerful!* the waves crashed against the little boat, the disciples were terrified, but Jesus slept in the midst of the tempest. When He was awakened, Jesus stood and commanded, *"Peace, be still!"* His disciples were awestruck. They *"feared exceedingly, and said to one another, 'Who can this be, that even the wind and the sea obey Him!'"* (see Mark 4:41).

The disciples knew the story of creation well. Who indeed was this Man who spoke, "Shalom" to calm the storm? None other than the Prince of Peace spoken of by Isaiah! (See Isaiah 9:6-7.) The Hebrew word for peace is *shalom*. The *shalom* of God includes wholeness, peace, health and healing, welfare, safety, salvation, deliverance, soundness, prosperity, perfectness, fullness, rest, harmony, no injustice, and no pain. Peace is the *essence* of the elusive abundant life promised by Jesus! "Prince of Peace" in Hebrew is *Sar Shalom*[1] meaning "the One who commands and has absolute control of peace."

At the time of creation, Jesus simply spoke and "the perfect harmony of His voice set the entire universe in place with the thundering words, "Let there be...."[2] The particles of the created universe came into harmony with God, order came, and peace reigned! The Prince of Peace is the Creator and Sustainer, still holding the vast expanse of the universe together—planets, stars, nebulae, solar systems, and galaxies—together. Our solar system consists of our sun, orbiting planets, moons, asteroids, rocks, and dust. Our sun is just one star among hundreds of billions of stars within the Milky Way Galaxy. A galaxy consists of many solar systems. The universe contains billions of galaxies beyond our own, stretching into the distant reaches of observable space into far reaches of the unknown.[3] If Jesus ever stopped holding all things together with the powerful word of His peace the universe would explode back into chaos (see Hebrews 1:3). He has authority over the wind, waves, and elements both then and now. If Jesus ever stopped speaking *shalom*, the universe would explode back into chaos. Jesus holds together and sustains all things (present tense: even right now) with His word of peace.

Jesus holds all things together with His word of peace.

...[Jesus] *created the worlds and the reaches of space and the ages of time.... He is the perfect imprint and very image of [God's] nature, upholding and maintaining and guiding and propelling the universe by His mighty word of power...* (Hebrews 11:2-3 AMPC).

When we understand the authority of Jesus as the Prince of Peace, His words take on a much more profound meaning: *"My peace I give to you."*

NOTES

1. We have a CD teaching on *Sar Shalom* that is available on our website, www .forgive123.com.

2. Michael Fickess, *Paths of Ever-Increasing Glory*, (Fort Mill, SC: MorningStar Publications, Inc., 2016), 71.

3. "Solar system, galaxy, universe: What's the difference?" *NASA Night Sky Network*, June 2017; https://nightsky.jpl.nasa.gov/news-display.cfm?News_ ID=573 accessed November 6, 2017.

CHAPTER 2

WHY ARE WE HERE?

Man's main concern is not to gain pleasure or to avoid pain but rather to see a meaning in his life.—Victor Frankl

One of the questions most frequently asked by Christians is, "What is God's plan for my life?" To answer that question, we must start with God, not us. Even if we were a surprise to our parents, the Lord wasn't surprised. No one ever came into the world by mistake. God Himself placed that question in our hearts because He fashioned us with destiny in mind.

Famed Austrian psychiatrist and holocaust survivor Victor Frankl (1905–1997) devoted his life to the study of *meaning*. During World War II, Frankl spent three years in Nazi death camps. His best-selling memoir, *Man's Search for Meaning*, has enthralled generations with graphic descriptions of the barbarity of life in concentration camps and what he learned about spiritual survival. It has been listed among the ten most influential books ever written.[1]

God fashioned us with destiny in mind.

By the time of Frankl's death, *Man's Search for Meaning* had sold more than ten million copies and had been translated into 24 different languages. In it, Frankl describes his quest for purpose in life and how it gave him both the will to live and the ability to overcome suffering. He developed his theory of psychoanalysis based on his belief that the discovery and pursuit of *meaning*, not pleasure, is our primary drive in life.

Your life story didn't start with your choice to believe in Jesus. God planned you when He purposed the way of redemption through the death and resurrection of His Son, Jesus. Before the universe was created, God held you in His heart and, when the time was right, placed you in your mother's womb:

Meaning is our primary drive in life.

> *You saw me before I was born. Every day of my life was recorded in your book. Every moment was laid out before a single day had passed"* (Psalm 139:16 NLT).

> *It's in Christ that we find out who we are and what we are living for. Long before we first heard of Christ…he had his eye on us, had designs on us for glorious living, part of the overall purpose he is working out in everything and everyone* (Ephesians 1:11 MSG).

God created us for:

- **Relationship:** *I will be a Father to you, and you shall be My sons and daughters, says the Lord Almighty* (2 Corinthians 6:18).

- **Pleasure:** *Thou art worthy, O Lord, to receive glory and honour and power: for thou hast created all things, and for thy pleasure they are and were created* (Revelation 4:11 KJV). *For the Lord takes pleasure in His people…* (Psalm 149:4).

- **Christ-Likeness:** *Throw off your old sinful nature and your former way of life, which is corrupted by lust and deception. Instead, let the Spirit renew your thoughts and attitudes. Put on your new nature, created to be like God—truly righteous and holy* (Ephesians 4:22-24 NLT).

- **Glory:** Thus says the Lord, *"Bring My sons from afar, and My daughters from the ends of the earth—everyone who is called by My name, whom I created for My glory…"* (Isaiah 43:6-7).

- **Purpose:** *For we are God's masterpiece. He has created us anew in Christ Jesus, so we can do the good things he planned for us long ago* (Ephesians 2:10 NLT).

A LIFE THAT COUNTS

People generally think about God's will only in terms of their own life. However, the true reason we're here is not just about personal success and happiness. It's much bigger than that. When we enter into the Lord's purpose for us, our life transcends earthly time and takes on eternal significance. Our life can become a life that counts for eternity!

> *…God has…planted eternity in the human heart* (Ecclesiastes 3:11 AMPC).

When we choose God's plan for our life, it's no longer just *my* life, *my* goals, and *my* success. Although we still make decisions—find a church home, go to school, get a job, get married—we enter into something far bigger than ourselves. When our *me-story* becomes part of *God's story*, it completely changes our view of life.

God knows you better than you know yourself. Have you ever wanted something

When our me-story *becomes part of* God's story, *it completely changes our view of life.*

very badly, yet, when you owned it, you felt dissatisfied? The new car smell dissipates, a new house grows old, appliances wear out, exciting new jobs lose their thrill, and relationships can sour. In the eyes of the world, King Solomon had it all—luxury, power, prestige, wisdom, women, education, and long life. Yet, in the book of Ecclesiastes, Solomon's search for meaning in life sounds a note of despair.

> *Smoke, nothing but smoke.... There's nothing to anything— it's all smoke. What's there to show for a lifetime of work, a lifetime of working your fingers to the bone? One generation goes its way, the next one arrives, but nothing changes—it's business as usual for old planet earth* (Ecclesiastes 1:2-4 MSG).

The phrase "under the sun" is used 29 times in Ecclesiastes and nowhere else in the Bible. It refers to the emptiness of earth-bound activities, acquisitions, or accomplishments when separated from God. There is no lasting value in life "under the sun." A life lived apart from God's will is filled with emptiness: *"My days are like a shadow that lengthens, and I wither away like grass"* (Psalm 102:11). And: *"For what will it profit a man if he gains the whole world, and loses his own soul?"* (Mark 8:36).

The true purpose of life is found in knowing God—life "over the sun" (see Galatians 2:20; Hebrews 2:10). G. Campbell Morgan (1863–1945), British evangelist, preacher and a leading Bible scholar, writes:

> This man [Solomon] had been living through all these experiences under the sun, concerned with nothing above the sun...until there came a moment in which he had seen the whole of life. And there was something over the sun. It is only as man takes account of that which is over

the sun as well as that which is under the sun that things under the sun are seen in their true light.[2]

Solomon concludes his quest with these words:

All has been heard; the end of the matter is: Fear God [revere and worship Him…] and keep His commandments, for this is…the full, original purpose of his creation…and the whole [duty] for every man (Ecclesiastes 12:13 AMPC).

The life Jesus lived is our example. He lived wholly to do His Father's will and, with that commitment, came the oil of gladness (see Psalm 45:7; Hebrews 1:9). Oswald Chambers writes:

What was the joy that Jesus had? Joy should not be confused with happiness. In fact, it is an insult to Jesus Christ to use the word happiness in connection with Him. The joy of Jesus was His absolute self-surrender and self-sacrifice to His Father—the joy of doing that which the Father sent Him to do—*"…who for the joy that was set before Him endured the cross…"* (Hebrews 12:2). *"I delight to do Your will, O my God…"* (Psalm 40:8). Jesus prayed that our joy might continue fulfilling itself until it becomes the same joy as His.[3]

JOY INEXPRESSIBLE

While Paul was a prisoner in a Roman jail awaiting execution, he wrote what is called the joy book of the Bible—the book of Philippians. In it, Paul uses the word *joy* 59 times and *rejoice* 74 times. Paul's secret was that he had given his life away and now lived for the will of God. Peter wrote to persecuted Christians, *"Though now you do not see Him, yet believing, you rejoice with joy inexpressible and full of glory"* (1 Peter 1:8).

Joy is a gift from God that overflows in those who live for Him. Although most American believers will never face persecution or imprisonment for their faith, we are offered the chance to partake of a joy that surpasses circumstances and even death—the joy of doing God's will.

> If I were looking for God, every event and every moment would sow, in my will, grains of His life that would spring up one day in a tremendous harvest…. It is God's love that speaks to me in the birds and streams; but also behind the clamor of the city God speaks to me in His judgments, and all of these things are seeds sent to me from His will. If these seeds would take root…I would become the love that He is, and my harvest would become His glory and my own joy…. And by accepting all things from Him, I receive His joy into my soul, not because things are what they are but because God is Who He is, and His love has willed my joy in them all.[4]

When God's will is done on earth, the Kingdom of God advances. What is the evidence that God's will is being done? *"The kingdom of God is righteousness* [God's love in action]…*peace and joy in the Holy Spirit"* (Romans 14:17). True peace and joy are discovered in doing God's will. Peace on earth as well as in our life is possible only through the government of God, which is the result of God's will being done.

Joy is a gift from God that overflows in those who live for Him.

> *…I will make peace your governor and well-being your ruler. No longer will violence be heard in your land, nor ruin or destruction within your borders, but you will call your walls Salvation and your gates Praise* (Isaiah 60:17-18 NIV).

PUT GOD FIRST

When we truly want the will of God for our lives and stay in communion with Him, He will put *His* desires in our hearts. *"Delight yourself also in the Lord, and He shall give you the desires of your heart"* (Psalm 37:4). As we delight in God, we want His will more than getting our own way. To wholeheartedly pursue the will of God, we must:

- Choose God's will over our own
- Trust God
- Take small steps of obedience
- Be patient and wait for God's timing
- Persevere

God will put **His** *desires in our hearts.*

STEP-BY-STEP

God *wants* you to live out your destiny. He has not hidden it from you. However, He reveals it step-by-step as you walk in obedience. Although the Lord may give us promises as He did Abraham, He lets us know what we need to know when we need to know it in a journey of discovery. The purpose of this book is to reveal how to move into destiny in effortless trust and perfect peace. It's as simple as that. That doesn't mean you won't endure some hardships or delays, but you can remain serene with the tangible assurance of God's presence.

Because we don't know what the future holds and life is full of surprises, we can only live in the present. Every moment is an opportunity we can claim for good or evil based on our response. Every moment is also a test. Therefore, Paul exhorts us, *"Live purposefully…making the very most of the time [buying up each opportunity]"* (Ephesians 5:15-16 AMPC).

Every moment is an opportunity we can claim for good.

God uses life to teach us trust. The Lord may give us some promises and prophetic glimpses but we can never know how it will all work out in the end. If He allows us to know too much, we would surely make a mess of it! Jesus reassures us that He cares about the details of our lives and that we can indeed trust Him. Spend some time meditating on the quality of life He offers us in the following passage of Scripture.

If you decide for God, living a life of God-worship, it follows that you don't fuss about what's on the table at mealtimes or whether the clothes in your closet are in fashion. There is far more to your life than the food you put in your stomach, more to your outer appearance than the clothes you hang on your body. Look at the birds, free and unfettered, not tied down to a job description, careless in the care of God. And you count far more to him than birds.

God uses life to teach us trust.

Has anyone by fussing in front of the mirror ever gotten taller by so much as an inch? All this time and money wasted on fashion—do you think it makes that much difference? Instead of looking at the fashions, walk out into the fields and look at the wildflowers. They never primp or shop, but have you ever seen color and design quite like it? The ten best-dressed men and women in the country look shabby alongside them.

If God gives such attention to the appearance of wildflowers—most of which are never even seen—don't you think he'll attend to you, take pride in you, do his best for you? **What I'm trying to do here is to get you to relax.**... *Steep your life in God-reality, God-initiative, God-provisions.*

Don't worry about missing out. You'll find all your everyday human concerns will be met.

Give your entire attention to what God is doing right now, and don't get worked up about what may or may not happen tomorrow. God will help you deal with whatever hard things come up when the time comes (Matthew 6:25-34 MSG).

PRINCE OF PEACE

When Jesus is in control, we are at peace because *"He Himself is our peace"* (Ephesians 2:14). Peace is evidence that we are under the lordship of Jesus. How do we know He is Lord in any given situation? Peace. When we are in control, we *lose* our peace because our heart *disconnects* from the Prince of Peace.

Let the peace of God rule in your hearts (Colossians 3:15).

The Bible likens peace to a great river that flows directly from Heaven, into our hearts, and, from there, out to the world: *"I will extend peace…like a river"* (Isaiah 66:12). We experience this peace only in the river of God's will. When we go against His flow, our hearts are troubled (see Isaiah 48:22). God created us for peace. Our spirits, souls, and bodies crave peace. No one in their right mind would deliberately choose turbulence and chaos over peace.

When we are saved, we become citizens of Heaven—children of another world (see Philippians 3:20). Heaven is now our true home. We find genuine satisfaction only when we are connected with the *atmosphere* of Heaven. Dan Delzell writes in *The Christian Post*, "Therefore, we need 'the river of heaven' to

Jesus brought the river of Heaven to our doorstep.

flow down and sweep us up in its peace and joy. When Jesus came into our world, He brought that river right to our doorstep."[5]

NOTES

1. Esther B. Fein, "Book Notes," *The New York Times*, November 20, 1991; http://www.nytimes.com/1991/11/20/books/book-notes-059091.html; accessed May 22, 2012.

2. G. Campbell Morgan, *The Unfolding Message of the Bible* (Oxford, UK: Cross-Reach Publications, 2017; first published 1961).

3. Oswald Chambers, "My joy...Your Joy," *Standing for God*, August 31, 2010; https://standingforgod.com/2010/08/31/my-joy-your-joy/#more-3454 accessed December 8, 2017.

4. Thomas Merton, *New Seeds of Contemplation* (Boston, MA: Shambhala Publications, Inc., 2003), 18–20.

5. Dan Delzell, "How to Have Peace Like a River," *The Christian Post*, May 2, 2013; http://www.christianpost.com/news/how-to-have-peace-like-a-river-94945/; accessed June 10, 2017.

CHAPTER 3

FLOWING IN PEACE

By Dennis

The mighty river released from Heaven to earth is supernatural power that gives peace to all who enter its flow. It is the river of God's will rushing down to us. The will of God is not *just* a plan or a blueprint, but waters of life that are ever-moving. It offers both the thrill of adventure and peace to all who enter its flow. Life in the river of peace is lived in union with the Prince of Peace. Jesus Himself *is* our peace and He is always with us (see Ephesians 2:14). He gave us His peace as a gift so it's always available. He never withdraws this marvelous gift of peace!

> **God's will grants peace to all who enter its flow.**

> *Peace I leave with you, My peace I give to you; not as the world gives do I give to you. Let not your heart be troubled, neither let it be afraid* (John 14:27).

PEACE IN OUR HEART

In the process of discovering God's will, we must begin with our *heart*. We encounter the river of peace in our heart. It's not a mental concept but an experience to be enjoyed in fellowship with the Lord. Our inner life is far more important to God than anything we do for Him. Our relationship with Him is the only gift we can give Him. Love God and make Him your top priority. He is a Person who wants to have a real relationship with you. Spend time in prayer with Him. Honor Him. Worship Him. Cultivate an awareness of His presence during the day. It is easier than you think when you realize that He is not just beside us but *inside*, in our heart (see Colossians 1:27).

Peace is evidence that we are in the river. When we lose our peace, we need to restore our relationship to enjoy peace once again. If we learn the lesson of peace well, we have found the key for abundant life because *"everything will live wherever the river goes"* (Ezekiel 47:9).

The river of peace is a supernatural force that sweeps us into destiny.

CHRIST IN US

Paul prayed that the nature of Christ would be formed within us (see Galatians 4:19). As believers, we are called to walk worthy of the One we represent (see Colossians 1:10). Who we are in our hearts is displayed in our character and behavior: *"Guard your heart above all else, for it determines the course of your life"* (Proverbs 4:23 NLT). When Philip asked Jesus, *"Show us the Father,"* Jesus replied, *"He who has seen Me has seen the Father"* (John 14:8-9).

Christ-like character in our hearts is formed through:

- The ministry of the Holy Spirit (John 14:26; Heb. 12:11)

- The truth of the Bible (2 Timothy 3:16)

- The people and circumstances of life (Colossians 1:11; Psalm 119:67,71)

- The grace of God (1 Corinthians 15:10)

THE NECESSITY OF OBEDIENCE

To maintain peace, we must also be obedient about what we know to do. The Lord does not make it mysterious or hard to know His will because life is always lived in the *now*. Our life is lived moment-by-moment and step-by-step. The grace of God is power for obedience: *"It is God who works in you both to will and to do for His good pleasure"* (Philippians 2:13).

If God does the "willing" and the "doing," what is our part? Yielding our hearts to Him. We get out of the way by surrendering to the Lord in our hearts and allowing Him to live through us: *"It is no longer I who live, but Christ lives in me"* (Galatians 2:20).

> *The grace of God is power for obedience.*

The Scriptures tell us almost all we need to know for everyday life: *"Your word is a lamp to my feet and a light to my path"* (Psalm 119:105). Our faithfulness is tested in small things in moments of time (Luke 19:17). Love and trust God. Be kind to people. Don't gossip. Fear not. Children, honor your parents. Husband, love your wife. Wife, respect your husband. Be a cheerful giver. Go to church (see Hebrews 10:25). That takes care of 90 percent of life.

However, we must not try to live by a set of rules in our own strength. The Pharisees in the Bible were rebuked by Jesus for striving to do just that. They had an external form of religion without intimacy with the Lord: *"You search the Scriptures because you think they give you eternal life. But the Scriptures point to me! Yet you refuse to come to me to receive this life"* (John 5:39-40 NLT).

When we are at peace, we have an assurance that we are walking in the light, and the light of the Lord will *"guide us to the path of peace"* (Luke 1:79 NLT). That doesn't mean that God won't give us more light later, but our obedience allows us to be confident in peace.

The [uncompromisingly] righteous [obedient] shall be glad in the Lord and shall trust and take refuge in Him; and all the upright in heart shall glory and offer praise (Psalm 64:10 AMPC).

GOD'S GUIDANCE

In addition to obeying the general precepts found in the Bible, specific guidance comes from *within*—in the form of increased anointing and inner assurance when all is going well or a sense of unease in our spirit when we need to make an adjustment. God wants to communicate with us. Jesus assures us that His sheep can hear His voice (see John 10: 3-16). Therefore, we must learn how to listen.

Some of the ways the Lord speaks include:

- The Bible (see 2 Timothy 3:16; Psalm 119:11,105)
- The still, small voice of the Holy Spirit (see Acts 16:6-7; 1 Kings 19:12-14)
- Creation and the natural world (see Romans 1:20)
- The audible voice of God (see Acts 9:4-5)
- Dreams and visions (see Matthew 1:20-21; Acts 10:9-18)
- Angels (see Luke 1:26-38; Acts 8:26)
- Circumstances and apparent coincidences (see Genesis 24:14-16)
- Inner assurance and peace (Romans 8:16; Acts 27:10-13; Colossians 3:15)
- An inner "no" of the Spirit (see Acts 16:6)
- People (see Acts 9:17)

- Revelation and illumination (see 2 Corinthians 4:6; Ephesians 3:3; Galatians 1:12)

What about life's big decisions? If we sincerely *want* to know, the Lord will reveal what we should do. Big decisions require big guidance. If we have inquiring hearts, we will get the answers we need.

RIVERS OF LIVING WATER

When I (Dennis) was a new believer, prayer was time spent with a Person, not just talking. When I closed my eyes to pray, I felt the closeness of His presence. Prayer was communing with Jesus and enjoying His nature. I set my heart to learn the *nuances* of God's "voice," but not just in words or verses from the Bible. In prayer, I paid close attention to the impressions I sensed in His presence. Sometimes I felt His acceptance and tender affection. At other times, I enjoyed the effervescence of His joy.

One time in particular when He brought the phrase "rivers of water" to mind, the anointing increased dramatically. At first, I responded by preaching to God all I knew about rivers in the Bible, but noticed that the anointing quickly dissipated. Soon I learned that I should wait and hear what God wanted to teach me. In this case, He was teaching me about living in the river of His peace: *"He who believes in Me, as the Scripture has said, out of his heart will flow **rivers of living water**"* (John 7:38).

God wants to communicate with us.

Once, while I was enjoying my time in prayer, the face of my foreman at my place of work flashed in my mind. The sensation in my gut surprised me by changing from pleasure to irritation. It didn't feel like the divine nature now! Somehow I had an understanding that it was wrong to hold an offense in my heart, so I presented the toxic emotion to Jesus. As I yielded to Him, without realizing what was happening, the Forgiver in me released a river of loving forgiveness through me toward my boss. When I opened my heart, forgiveness washed the bad feeling out, and I immediately experienced the comfort of God's presence return. The Lord spoke to my heart, "Don't let anything come between what you and I have together!" How to forgive and have peace with God restored proved to be one of the most valuable lessons I ever learned.

Living in the river of peace became a lifestyle. It is the way of Life and the secret for abiding in the Vine. *"I am the vine, you are the branches. He who abides in Me, and I in him, bears much fruit; for without Me you can do nothing"* (John 15:5). When our heart stays open to Jesus, His life flows through our life. When we open our heart toward other people, that same river flows out as forgiveness, when needed, or love toward others in loving intercession.

Living in the river of peace is a lifestyle.

It was a simple yet profound concept. From this time on, peace became a tutor that kept me in the will of God.

GUIDED BY PEACE

My fellowship with the Lord was marked by the exhilarating joy of fellowship with the Lord. For six months after my baptism in the Holy Spirit, the joy was so strong that it felt like my skin would explode, but I didn't care because it was so glorious. *"You feed them from the abundance of your own house, letting them drink from your **river of delights**"* (Psalm 36:8 NLT). God's will *contains* His pleasure: *"In Your presence is fullness of joy"* (Psalm 16:11).

Because God created us for His pleasure, it is right that we should experience joy in His presence. *"Thou art worthy, O Lord, to receive glory and honour and power: for thou hast created all things, and for thy pleasure they are and were created"* (Revelation 4:11 KJV).

Everything the Lord revealed, I cherished in my heart like pure gold. Every word the Lord speaks is alive and grows. Over time, by holding the precious nuggets God gave me in my heart, they grew and bore fruit in my life. Some grew into guidance for decisions. Others grew into sermons. Still others were used by God to minister to specific individuals.

In everyday life, the Lord guides us by His peace. *"He Himself is our peace"* (Ephesians 1:27). When we have peace in our heart, we are walking in the light that we have. We should walk confidently and be obedient to what we know. If we need to change our direction, our peace will first be interrupted, then restored as we alter our course. If we need to wait, we'll sense it. When we need light for the next step, He'll give it to us. *"The path of the just is like the shining sun, that shines ever brighter unto the perfect day"* (Proverbs 4:18).

Rest in the flow of God's peace.

To stay in God's will, we must flow *with* the Lord rather than swim against the current. When we rest in the flow of His peace, the river takes us where He wants us to go. The will of God ceases to be mysterious because He is the river with whom we flow.

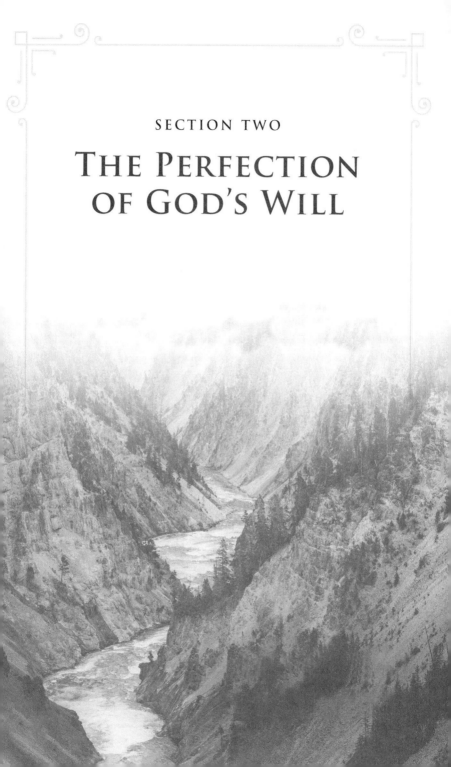

SECTION TWO

THE PERFECTION
OF GOD'S WILL

CHAPTER 4

UNDERSTANDING GOD'S WILL

By Jennifer

The subject of the will of God can be a challenge to understand based on terminology alone. Throughout the centuries, terms such as *sovereign will, moral will, efficient will, permissive will, secret will, revealed will, will of decree, will of command, decretive will, voluntas signi* (will of sign), *voluntas beneplaciti* (will of good pleasure), *efficacious will,* and so forth, have been endlessly debated.

To simplify the subject, we can easily understand the will of God based on three aspects clearly revealed in Scripture—eternal, moral, and specific.

- **God's Eternal Purpose**
  God has an eternal purpose that was conceived in eternity past and will come to completion in eternity future. Only God understands it completely, but He has a plan for humankind and the universe that will happen without fail. *He does according to his will in the host of heaven and among the inhabitants of the earth* (Daniel 4:35 AMPC).
  The book of Ephesians reveals that God's eternal purpose includes an intention, God's will, with a goal and a means of accomplishing that plan according to *"the eternal*

purpose which He accomplished in Christ Jesus our Lord"
(Ephesians 3:11). Because Ephesians was written from
the perspective of God, it specifically addresses God's will,
counsel, purpose, and means of bringing it to completion.
"If we study Ephesians with a spirit of revelation, we will
realize that the aim of God's plan is to have an expression of Himself in Christ the Son by the Spirit through a
Body composed and built up with many regenerated and
transformed people [the sons of God] by the mingling of
Himself with humanity."[1]

- **God's Moral Will**
  God's moral will is not secret and is the same for everyone.
  It is God's will for human conduct and includes His
  commandments, prohibitions, and principles. He has
  revealed it in the Bible, and we are expected to learn it,
  accept it, and obey it. We can simplify the meaning of
  "sin" in terms of God's moral will: When we sin, we miss
  the mark of the loving and wise will of God.
  *Whoever has my commandments and keeps them is the one
  who loves me* (John 14:21 NIV).

- **God's Specific Will**
  God has a unique purpose for each individual and will
  reveal it to us *as we seek Him*. We are created with a will to
  make decisions about our life so we can either choose or
  reject God's plan for us.
  The Lord will work out his plans for my life (Psalm 138:8 NLT).

WHAT ABOUT FREE WILL?

God has given us the ability to make decisions. If we couldn't
make choices we would be like robots. However, God wants a real
relationship with us. He wants us to love Him and choose to be
part of His family—but we can say, "No." After Jesus offended
many would-be followers by saying they must eat His flesh and

drink His blood, *"many of His disciples went back and walked with Him no more. Then Jesus said to the twelve, "Do you also **want** to go away?"* (John 6:66-67). Jesus also asked the sick man lying at the pool of Bethesda, *"Do you **want** to be made well?"* (John 5:6).

So what does it mean that we have a *free will?* We can obey God a little bit but not fully. However, He is not pleased with partial obedience. Consider King Saul. In 1 Samuel chapter 15, Saul is commanded by God to annihilate the Amalekites and all their livestock (1 Sam. 15:3). However, Saul had another idea. He spared the life of King Agag as well as the lives of the best of the sheep, cattle, calves, and lambs.

As we can clearly see, partial obedience is really disobedience...and the consequences in this case were severe. The prophet Samuel delivered the word of the Lord to Saul, *"The Lord has torn the kingdom of Israel from you today and has given it to someone else—one who is better than you"* (1 Samuel 15:28 NLT).

During World War II, the nation of Switzerland refused to take sides in the conflict and declared itself to be "neutral." The warring nations respected that decision and left Switzerland alone. We do not have a free will that can be independent in this way. Our will is free only to the extent that we can choose to submit to God or the devil. *"Do you not know that to whom you present yourselves slaves to obey, you are that one's slaves whom you obey, whether of sin leading to death, or of obedience leading to righteousness?"* (Romans 6:16). Therefore, we can only submit our will to one of two laws: the law of sin and death or the law of the Spirit of Life in Christ Jesus (see Romans 8:2).

Partial obedience is disobedience!

And you He made alive, who were dead in trespasses and sins, in which you once walked according to the course of *this world, according to **the prince of the power of the air, the spirit who now works in the sons of disobedience*** (Ephesians 2:1-2).

Now he who keeps His commandments abides in Him, and He in him. *And by this we know that He abides in us, by the Spirit whom He has given us* (1 John 3:24).

PROMPT OBEDIENCE

The most important thing about knowing God's will for our lives is to make a decision in advance to *do* it once we *know* it. (If you ever feel stuck about guidance for the next step in your life, make sure you did the last thing God told you.) When the Lord gives us a specific command, He doesn't factor procrastination into it. Even if you don't understand the reasoning, obey quickly. If you need more information later, God will let you know.

When we moved into a new church building a number of years ago, the Lord gave me (Dennis) a series of small assignments that seemed a bit silly, such as hanging a plaque with grapes in the kitchen. Later, He let me know the prophetic meaning of each step and told me that I had passed His test.

If we are obedient in small things, God can trust us with big things.

If we are obedient in small things, God can safely entrust us with big things. *"If you are faithful in little things, you will be faithful in large ones. But if you are dishonest in little things, you won't be honest with greater responsibilities"* (Luke 16:10 NLT).

NOTE

1. Witness Lee, *General Sketch of the New Testament, A-Pt. 2*; http://www.ministry samples.org/excerpts/Gods-eternal-purpose-and-economy.html; accessed June 11, 2017.

CHAPTER 5

WE CAN'T KNOW IT ALL

Never be afraid to trust an unknown future to a known God.
—Corrie Ten Boom

Even when we don't know we need protection, God protects us. He knows what is just around the bend. We won't know all the times God kept us safe without our knowledge until we are in Heaven; but every once in a while, we get a glimpse of how much we need Him. Jen and I (Dennis) were returning from a ministry trip in the northeast. It was just the sort of drive we enjoy—perfect weather, light traffic, and no road construction delays so far.

GOD HOLDS THE FUTURE

We were headed south in heavily mountainous terrain on Interstate 77 in the Fancy Gap area of the Smoky Mountains near Hillsville, Virginia. This particular section of highway makes a steep southbound descent with a grade of around five percent for the last four miles. Toward the east, a rocky cliff drops off into a beautiful valley with mountains to the east. As we rounded a curve on the highway, traffic came to a sudden and complete standstill. Uh, oh!

Wondering what might be causing the delay, we glanced at the metal guard rail and steep cliff on our left and joked about the runaway truck ramp to our right, access to which was now blocked by a line of idling cars. We couldn't see far ahead but speculated that a traffic accident or road work might be to blame. It was curious that our car and the one to our right were the last cars in our respective lanes so, whatever the cause, traffic had got backed up fairly recently. Our hearts were at peace despite the inconvenience of a delay.

Suddenly, I obeyed an inner prompting to move over into the right lane although it made no logical sense. However, as soon as we moved over, I glanced in the rearview mirror and my eyes widened. With smoking tires and sparks flying from metal-on-metal impact, a massive truck barreled toward our now-vacated left lane position, plowing into the guard rail. Only the now-twisted rail prevented it from ramming into the line of cars straight ahead as it screeched to a halt. If we had remained in the left lane, we would have been completely crushed.

It was clear that we had escaped an almost certain death!

TRUST, LISTEN, OBEY

Our life is held in the hands of the One who holds the future. God knows everything. We only know in part. The Lord reveals what we need to know when we need to know it. We listen to Him and act in obedience. When we are obedient to the last thing He told us, God tells us the next step. The process goes like this: trust-listen-obey. God orders our steps as we trust in Him.

> Our preoccupation with what lies ahead betrays a desire to control a future that simply can't be controlled. We want the security of knowing what the future will bring rather than risk trusting God as the unknown future gradually

unfolds before us. We keep hoping the light will shine to illumine the entire journey ahead so that we will know everything there is to know about the future, and thus be spared the difficulty of having to trust God. Ironically, we want to know so much about the future that we won't even have to trust God anymore.[1]

If God told us everything, we wouldn't need to trust Him. When we believe in our heart that God is both good and faithful, we can trust Him with an unknown future. *"'I know the plans that I have for you,' declares the Lord, 'plans for welfare and not for calamity to give you a future and a hope'"* (Jeremiah 29:11 NASB).

We can trust God with an unknown future.

Discovering God's will is a way of life. A way of life? What does that mean? Living a life surrendered to God. When Jesus is Lord of our lives, He leads us. We yield control and He takes over. Why is Psalm 23 about the Shepherd and His sheep so comforting? Because this world often seems scary and uncertain. Most of us would admit we like the idea of Someone looking out for us! The sheep stay close to the Shepherd—He leads them and cares for them even when they don't even recognize the perils at every hand.

Discovering God's will is a way of life.

Start with Your Heart

In seeking God's will, start with your *heart*. Life is far more about feelings than logic, not that our reasoning mind isn't important, but because we ultimately choose according to desire. God responds to our heart. When we draw close to Him, we sense that He is with us. *"Draw near to God and He will draw near to you"* (James 4:8).

"Draw near to God."

What happens in our heart? All spiritual reality is revealed to the *heart*, before it can be understood in the head. No wonder we are admonished to pay careful attention to what goes on in our heart (see Proverbs 4:23). According to the Scriptures:

- Salvation happens in the heart. *"For with the heart one believes"* (Romans 10:10).

- Love for God comes from the heart. *"[L]ove the Lord your God with all your heart"* (Deuteronomy 6:5). *"You shall love the Lord your God with all your heart"* (Matthew 22:37).

- Faith arises in the heart. *"Let us draw near with a true heart in full assurance of faith"* (Hebrews 10:22).

- Anointing flows from the heart. *"He that believeth on me, as the scripture hath said, out of his belly shall flow rivers of living water. (But this spake he of the Spirit, which they that believe on him should receive)"* (John 7:38-39 KJV).

- Trust is established in the heart. *"Trust in the Lord with all your heart"* (Proverbs 3:5).

- The Word of God is planted in the heart. *"[H]umbly accept the word God has planted in your hearts, for it has the power to save your souls"* (James 1:21 NLT).

- True forgiveness comes from the heart. *"[F]orgive…from your heart"* (Matthew 18:35 NLT).

- Christian fellowship is a matter of the heart. *"[B]e of one mind, having compassion for one another; love as brothers, be tenderhearted"* (1 Peter 3:8).

Our heart is the center of our inner life and contains the essence of who we are. Therefore, when we speak of knowing and doing God's will, we must always begin with the heart. *"When You said, 'Seek My face,' My heart said to You, 'Your face, Lord, I will seek'"* (Psalm 27:8). The epicenter of our spirit is located in our heart, as is our soul.

The soul consists of thoughts, will, and emotions (1 Thessalonians 5:23). Thoughts, will, and emotions in the soul can be carnal, ruled by our flesh, or submitted to the Holy Spirit. Human beings have both a soul and spirit because they are made in the image of God (see Genesis 1:26-27).[2] Our spirit makes it possible for us to discover God.

God is known and worshipped through the spirit. He communicates with us in the realm of the spirit. *"God is spirit, and those who worship Him must worship in spirit and truth"* (John 4:24). Because God is Spirit, He created man in His image as a spirit being. Our spirit allows us to become conscious of God. When we commune with God, our spirit touches His Spirit. We can contact God only by the spirit! If we didn't have a spirit, we wouldn't be able to know God. He is the *"Father of spirits"* (Hebrews 12:9). We are His spiritual children. *"The Spirit Himself bears witness with our spirit that we are children of God"* (Romans 8:16).

Before Adam and Eve sinned, their spirit and soul were perfectly aligned with God. Afterward, they were no longer attuned to God's thoughts, will, and emotions. Yes, God has emotions but His are *holy* emotions. God is an emotional God. He not only has emotions, but His very nature is emotional. God does not simply have love; He *is* love (see 1 John 4:8).

When Adam sinned, his spirit was separated from God. He died a spiritual death. Harmony between God and man was fractured. Adam became flesh-ruled rather than spirit-ruled. Man's fallen nature and God's heavenly nature no longer matched. Jesus died on the cross and paid the penalty for the sins of humankind through the shedding of His own blood. Because of the death, burial, and resurrection of Jesus, we can experience spiritual rebirth and enjoy communion with God. When we are born again, our ability to touch God in the spirit is restored (John 3:6).

When we commune with God, our spirit touches His Spirit.

[I]t is in our spirit that God dwells (Ephesians 2:22; 2 Timothy 4:22; Romans 8:16); it is in our spirit that we are joined to the Lord (1 Corinthians 6:17); and it is in our spirit that we contact and worship God (John 4:24). Now we must walk and have our whole being according to our spirit—serving in our spirit (Romans 1:9), praying in spirit (Ephesians 6:18), being filled in spirit (5:18), seeing God's revelation in spirit (1:17; 3:5; Revelation 1:10; 4:2; 17:3; 21:10), having fellowship with the brothers and sisters in spirit (Philippians 2:1), and being built together with others into a dwelling place of God in spirit (Ephesians 2:22).[3]

AWARENESS AND OBEDIENCE

To know God, spend time in prayer with Him. Honor Him. Worship Him. The first key to loving God is awareness. Cultivate an awareness of His presence. Become sensitive to His presence during the day.

When we focus on God in prayer, we touch Him spirit-to-Spirit. If you are driving a car and you have passengers in the back seat, you are conscious of their presence even if you can't see them.

Be aware of God. In the same way, we should live with a constant awareness of God by keeping our hearts open to Him all day long.

The second key to loving God is obedience to what we know to *do*. Obey God's moral will. Obey God's voice. When we do the last thing God told us, He will tell more. *"If anyone is willing to do His will, he will know"* (see John 7:17). Good character and obedience are more important than our gifts and talents. *"He has shown you, O man, what is good; and what does the Lord require of you but to do justly, to love mercy, and to walk humbly with your God?"* (Micah 6:8).

We simply need to do what we already know in the present. God has been clear where clarity is most needed. The choices we make every day…determine whether or not we are doing the will of God…. Who we choose to become and how we choose to live every day creates a trajectory for everything else. Perhaps that is why the Bible says so little about God's will for tomorrow and so much about what we should do to fulfill His will today.[4]

SECOND CHANCES

What if we make a mistake? Will we miss our destiny? Rest assured, if we do make a wrong decision now and then, or even take a long detour, the Lord is smart enough to fix our mistakes and get us back on track as we follow Him. Get back up and trust God. It is true that we may have to deal with the consequences of our actions, but the Lord is loving and merciful to those whose hearts are turned toward Him.

Perhaps you are afraid you'll make the wrong choices and miss out on God's best. Maybe things were going well but suddenly you find yourself at a critical decision point. Cheer up! Do you know how rare it is for *Be obedient to God.* someone to want God's will? That alone delights the heart of God. No one who truly wants to be obedient to the will of God will miss it in the long run.

God is the God of second chances…and third, fourth, and fifth. Life is not like baseball—three strikes and you're out. A lot of people in the Bible made mistakes and God didn't write *them* off. Moreover, some made blunders far worse than any you're likely to make. David committed adultery. Abraham traded his wife for personal safety. Sarah laughed at God's promises. Samson was a womanizer. Paul was a murderer.

Our son, Jason, took a twenty-year detour from God's will into sin and toxic relationships. Not only did God bring him back full-circle, but is using his testimony of God's amazing redemption to minister hope to others.[5] He is living proof that the Lord can deliver, heal, and give us a brand new start.

> *God made my life complete when I placed all the pieces before him. When I cleaned up my act, he gave me a fresh start. …God rewrote the text of my life when I opened the book of my heart to his eyes* (2 Samuel 22:21-25 MSG).

GOD CARES ABOUT DETAILS

Have you ever noticed that the details in the Scriptures are highly significant? More books have been written about the Bible than any other subject in history, yet its richness continues to be explored by scholars. Every word is meaningful. The consistency from Genesis to Revelation inspires awe, particularly when we consider that it was written by many different individuals under the inspiration of the Holy Spirit.

Why, then, should we be surprised that the Lord orders our lives with great care. As Jesus said to the disciples of old, so He speaks to us today:

> *Are not two sparrows sold for a copper coin? And not one of them falls to the ground apart from your Father's will. But the very hairs of your head are all numbered. Do not fear therefore; you are of more value than many sparrows* (Matthew 10:29-31).

When Jesus called the apostle Peter, he was casting a net into the sea to catch fish. Jesus told Peter He would make him a fisher of men (see Matthew 4:19). Peter used the keys of the Kingdom given to him by Jesus to open the Kingdom of Heaven, then threw out his net to draw in both Jew and Gentile (see Matthew 16:19; Acts 2:14-38; Acts 10:1-47).

John, the disciple whom Jesus loved, on the other hand, was in a boat mending nets when he was called by Jesus (see Matthew 4:21-22). What did Jesus tell Him to do when he was caught up in the Spirit on the isle of Patmos (see Revelation 2–3)? "Tell My churches their nets need to be mended!" In addressing the seven churches, Jesus said He knew their works, the challenges they were facing, and where they needed to repent. From first love that needed to be restored to repentance for indifference and worldliness, Jesus revealed their weak areas and told them how they would be rewarded for overcoming. Who better to transmit the messages than John, the mender of nets, who knew the heartbeat of His Master.

God orders our lives with great care.

Everything the Lord speaks to us has great significance and He does care about the details.

When our daughter was graduating from high school, we bought her a used car. Soon, however, I (Dennis) became concerned because of a problem with the transmission, and transmission repair can be expensive.

Suddenly a bottle of transmission fluid conditioner I had noticed when I had my last oil change, flashed into my mind. The Lord said, "Try that fluid." It cost less than ten dollars. After I added the fluid, she never had another problem with the car's transmission. In an area where I had no expertise, God was my Expert.

In another situation, I was shopping with Jen, and she wanted a particular new blouse. I felt a check in my Spirit to wait. A few days later, we found it on the clearance rack 75 percent off. We don't need to pray about every decision, but we do need to be open to God's guidance. How much guidance do we miss because we dismiss the leadings of the Spirit?

We need to be aware of God's guidance.

TRUSTING GOD

God is not far away. Let us emphasize again that we are God-indwelt: Christ *in us* is our hope of glory (see Colossians 1:27). Jesus tells us, *"The kingdom of God is within"* (Luke 17:21). Almost all of our *specific* guidance should come from *within*: as increased anointing and inner assurance when all is going well or a sense of unease in our spirit when we need to make an adjustment.

Although God may occasionally give us "signs" or external corroboration, we suggest that you be hesitant about using such techniques as "Bible-flop" (letting the Bible fall open and then pointing at a random verse) or using a "fleece" (if…happens, it means…) (see Judges 6:36-37).

When we are born again, we are brought into a union with a Living Person. We come to Jesus and receive Him as Life. *"It is no longer I who live, but Christ lives in me"* (Galatians 2:20). We are God-indwelt. Let us not make the same mistake made by the Galatians in the Bible. They had received *life* through the Spirit, but resorted to living by *willpower*. The Christian life is *trusting* not *trying!* Paul strongly rebuked the Galatian believers, saying:

> *Let me ask you this one question: Did you receive the Holy Spirit by obeying the law of Moses? Of course not! You received the Spirit because you believed the message you heard about Christ. How foolish can you be? After starting your new lives in the Spirit, why are you now trying to become perfect by your own human effort?* (Galatians 3:2-3 NLT)

What about the other ten percent of life where we *do* need God's specific guidance? The process of flowing in God's will happens in everyday living. This is where the river of God's peace comes in. We navigate the river by living in peace.

Because we have the life of the Holy Spirit within us, *"let us follow the Spirit's leading in every part of our lives"* (Galatians 5:25 NLT).

Live in effortless trust and perfect peace.

LIVING UNDER CONTROL

Jesus had just returned to Nazareth, His place of birth, after ministering in the cities around the Sea of Galilee. The boy next door was now quite a celebrity. When He entered the synagogue the following Sabbath, He was asked to read from the Torah and teach on the text.

Much to the astonishment of the townsfolk, Jesus read from Messianic prophecy of Isaiah 61:1-5 about the Spirit of the Lord anointing Him to preach the Gospel, heal the brokenhearted, and set the captives free. Then He announced, *"Today this Scripture is fulfilled in your hearing"* (Luke 4:21).

The people in attendance were enraged because He had called *Himself* the promised Messiah! This was blasphemy in their ears! How dare He! *"So all those in the synagogue, when they heard these things, were filled with wrath, and rose up and thrust Him out of the city; and they led Him to the brow of the hill on which their city was built, that they might throw Him down over the cliff"* (Luke 4:28-29).

Jesus didn't fight them, run from them, or let them shove Him off the cliff to His death. *"Passing through the midst of them, He went His way"* (Luke 4:30). He walked right through the crowd and no one laid a hand on Him. Jesus was one and they were many. Why didn't they just grab Him and stop Him?

Because Jesus was under His Father's control, they were unable to touch Him. It was not the will of the Father for Him to be harmed. It was not His time to die. Jesus was able to pass through the crowd because He was fully submitted to the will of His Father.

When we are submitted to the will of God, we too are under His control. When we are surrendered to Him, we can remain at peace and have an inner assurance that God is *God is in control.* in complete control of our lives—regardless of the circumstances of life.

NOTES

1. Jerry Sittser, *The Will of God as a Way of Life: How to Make Every Decision with Peace and Confidence* (Grand Rapids, MI: Zondervan, 2000, 2004), 27.

2. Humans are spirit beings who have souls (thoughts, will, and emotions) and live in bodies. (Animals consist of only soul and body.) God has given us the capacity to interact with the realm of the spirit and discover Him. When we are born again, our spirit is made alive unto God and can then commune with God's Spirit. Unsaved individuals also have spirits, but their spirits are "dead," or separated from God.

   Both believer and nonbeliever can have spiritual experiences. The question is, what spiritual realm is contacted—holy or evil? For those seeking deep spiritual experiences, or "transcendent states," there is a primary difference between *how* they seek and *what* they seek. Scientists have studied both Christians and non-Christians, people of many different religious persuasions, and found the neural evidence of a spiritual experience is very similar (when studied on brain scans). It should not be surprising that our spiritual capacity can be used both for good and for evil. However, when we come to God, we come in faith believing that we can safely open our heart to Him.

   > *If a son asks for bread from any father among you, will he give him a stone? Or if he asks for a fish, will he give him a serpent instead of a fish? Or if he asks for an egg, will he offer him a scorpion? If you then, being evil, know how to give good gifts to your children, how much more will your heavenly Father give the Holy Spirit to those who ask Him!* (Luke 11:11-13)

   The Christian approach is an active seeking with the intention to quiet the soul (carnal mind, will, and emotions), transcend self, and focus intently on a personal God. Thoughts, emotions, and perceptions are brought under the control of the Holy Spirit. The goal is drawing closer to the Lord. Self is not obliterated but yielded to God.

Followers of New Age and Eastern religions seek a state of pure awareness, or consciousness of "everything" as an undifferentiated whole through passive seeking. They attempt to have a blank mind so they can merge with "everything" and obliterate self. They do not seek a deity who is "out there" and separate from humankind. To them, god and the entire universe are part of a cosmic consciousness, or force, with which everything can merge, and become "no-thing," much like pureed vegetable soup.

3. Benson Phillips, *Foreword: Our Human Spirit*, originally from *The Collected Works of Witness Lee* (Anaheim, CA: Living Stream Ministry, 1963); https://www.ministrybooks.org/books.cfm?xid=0KVWYAADSIWSF; accessed May 18, 2015.

4. Sittser, *The Will of God as a Way of Life*, 25.

5. Jason's remarkable testimony, Grace Transforms, is available on our website www.forgive123.com in CD and DVD format. It is also available as an mp3 download at http://store.teamembassy.com.

CHAPTER 6

RELEASING HEAVEN ON EARTH

The human heart yearns for heaven. Even in this age of cynicism and skepticism, our heart cries out for something more than this earthly life of struggling, suffering, living and dying. We recoil from the idea that we might cease to exist and crave the assurance that we will live forever. The idea of heaven holds a special fascination for us and the vast majority of Americans want to go there. A 2016 Gallup poll found that 89 percent of Americans believe in God and 72 percent believe in the reality of heaven and angels.[1]

And what is heaven like? Pause for a moment and just imagine the bliss and perfection of heaven. It is the dwelling place of God Himself. Innumerable heavenly beings and angels rejoice and praise continually. Believers hold fast to the hope that they will someday join those who have passed on before: *"I looked, and behold, a great multitude which no one could number, of all nations, tribes, peoples, and tongues, standing before the throne and before the Lamb, clothed with white robes, with palm branches in their hands, and crying out with a loud voice, saying, 'Salvation belongs to our God who sits on the throne, and to the Lamb!'"* (Revelation 7:9-10).

Love and joy permeate the atmosphere. All tears are gone because no sadness or grief can exist there. *"God will wipe away every tear from their eyes; there shall be no more death, nor sorrow, nor crying. There shall be no more pain, for the former things have passed away"* (Revelation 2:14). Unlike earth, no violent catastrophes or tragic events can possibly occur.

Heaven is described as a realm of indescribable beauty and majesty. The Apostle John describes what he himself saw there:

The four living creatures, each having six wings, were full of eyes around and within. And they do not rest day or night, saying: Immediately I was in the Spirit; and behold, a throne set in heaven, and One sat on the throne. And He who sat there was like a jasper and a sardius stone in appearance; and there was a rainbow around the throne, in appearance like an emerald. Around the throne were twenty-four thrones, and on the thrones I saw twenty-four elders sitting, clothed in white robes; and they had crowns of gold on their heads. And from the throne proceeded lightnings, thunderings, and voices. Seven lamps of fire were burning before the throne, which are the seven Spirits of God.

Before the throne there was a sea of glass, like crystal. And in the midst of the throne, and around the throne, were four living creatures full of eyes in front and in back.... And they do not rest day or night, saying: "Holy, holy, holy, Lord God Almighty, Who was and is and is to come!" Whenever the living creatures give glory and honor and thanks to Him who sits on the throne, who lives forever and ever, the twenty-four elders fall down before Him who sits on the throne and worship Him who lives forever and ever, and cast their crowns before the throne (Revelation 4:2-6, 8-10).

John also tells us of streets of translucent gold, twelve gates of magnificent pearls, and twelve foundations made of precious jewels (see Revelation 21:14-21). *"And I saw no temple in the city, for its temple is the Lord God the Almighty and the Lamb. And the city has no need of sun or moon to shine on it, for the glory of God gives it light, and its lamp is the Lamb"* (Revelation 21:22-23). No created sources of light are necessary because heaven is illumined by the radiant glory of God and the Lamb!

We pray so fervently for revival because we long for God's presence and glory to invade earth. Revival is a foretaste of heaven come to earth.

THE PERFECTION OF GOD'S WILL

We all know that Heaven is very different from life on earth. But exactly what makes Heaven *Heaven?* Heaven is a realm filled with the love and glory of God, where God's will is perfectly obeyed. God's will is not just His commandments, ideas, or plans. It is the expression of Heaven's perfection, abounding with God's life and love and glory. It accomplishes His purposes for the highest good. The inhabitants of Heaven continuously rejoice as God's will is done.

> The glory and the blessedness of heaven consist of nothing but this—God's will is done therein and by all. There is nothing to hinder God's working His blessed will in countless hosts. Those to whom He wills goodness, blessedness, and service, surrender their whole being in submission and adoration. God lives in them and they in God. They are filled with the fullness of God. In the Lord's Prayer, our Blessed Master teaches us to come to the Father with the wonderful petition that His will may be done on earth, even "as it is in heaven"![2]

The will of God is a continual flow of His divine purposes. The Kingdom of God is the power and glory of Heaven released on earth. Jesus came to do His Father's will and expand the Kingdom of God on earth. Jesus told us to pray, *"Your kingdom come. Your will be done on earth as it is in heaven"* (Matthew 6:10). Christians are called to co-labor with God to advance God's kingdom to earth.

> *God's will is the expression of Heaven's perfection.*

In the will of God, we have the perfect expression of His divine perfection. Because He is the fountain of all beauty and blessedness, His will is inconceivably beautiful and blessed. His divine wisdom and goodness are made known through it. Through it alone can man know his God. In accepting and doing God's will, man finds the only and the sure way to fellowship and union with the Father.[3]

THE ETERNAL RIVER

God's will is released in a river of peace that flows from Genesis to Revelation, down through the ages, and springs up within our own hearts (see Genesis 2:10; Revelation 22:1-2). Everywhere peace flows, the Kingdom of God is established. Just as chaos was conquered by supernatural peace at the foundation of the world, peace still triumphs today.

The river of peace flows from Genesis to Revelation.

The book of Isaiah uses the word *shalom* 27 times, more than any other book in the Bible. The subject of peace begins with the Prince of Peace and His ever-increasing government and peace in Isaiah 9:6-7 and concludes with God's promise to *"extend peace like a river"* (Isaiah 66:12). "Extend" is the Hebrew word *natâh*, meaning to stretch, extend, expand. According to *New Wilson's Old Testament Word Studies*, "I will extend peace like a river" means *in the abundance and perpetuity of a full large river.*[4]

The Garden of Eden was created on earth as a frontier outpost of Heaven on earth. Eden was a dwelling place of God on earth where God communed with His children.[5] Out of Eden a river flowed and split into four riverheads to water the Garden.[6] The river is still available for us today.

In John 4:14, Jesus said to the woman at the well, *"Whoever drinks of the water that I shall give him will never thirst. But the water that I shall give him will become in him a fountain of water springing up into everlasting life.”* However, Jesus merely said that the *mayim chayim* (plural), living waters, gave everlasting life, *zoë,* but did not explain further until later.

> **“Whoever drinks of the water that I give shall never thirst.”**

In the temple during the Feast of Tabernacles, the feast celebrating God dwelling with His people, *“Jesus stood and said in a loud voice, ‘Let anyone who is thirsty come to me and drink. Whoever believes in me, as Scripture has said, rivers of living water will flow from within them.’ By this he meant the Spirit, whom those who believed in him were later to receive. Up to that time the Spirit had not been given, since Jesus had not yet been glorified”* (John 7:37-39 NIV).

The living waters, therefore, symbolize the Holy Spirit. Jesus promised that the same rivers that flowed in Eden would spring up in believers and flow out from God enthroned within their hearts. When we first turn from our sin and receive Jesus in our heart, we *connect* with the river of peace. The Lord begins the work of salvation in us. The Prince of Peace brings order into the chaos of our life. Every area where Jesus establishes His lordship, His peace replaces our disorder, fear, anger, disappointment, anxiety, lawlessness, and disharmony with God.

THE SOURCE OF THE RIVER

Jesus is both the Cornerstone and the Foundation Stone. As the Cornerstone, Jesus is the standard with which the living stones align as Christ builds His church (see Matthew 16:16-18), and He is the Rock, or Foundation, upon which His church is built (see Matthew 7:24-27).

As the Foundation Stone, He is the source of the living waters. Foundation Stone in Hebrew is *even ha-shetiyah.* This stone is also called *shetiyah,* which means “drinking” because Jewish tradition says the source of all underground springs and fountains in the world is hidden beneath it. A large wooden sign at the Wailing Wall in Jerusalem is entitled "The Divine Presence Never Moves from the Western Wall." It relates the Jewish belief that the Foundation Stone on the Temple Mount is the location of creation and that Jerusalem lies at the center of the world. On it are written these words:

> Jewish tradition teaches that the Temple Mount is the focal point of Creation. In the center of the mountain lies the "Foundation Stone" of the world. Here Adam came into being. Here Abraham, Isaac and Jacob served God. The First and Second Temples were built upon this mountain. The Ark of the Covenant was set upon the Foundation Stone itself. Jerusalem was chosen by God as the dwelling place of the Shechinah…. The Sages said about it: "The Divine Presence never moves from the Western Wall. The Temple Mount continues to be the focus of prayer for Jews from around the world."[7]

There is no spiritual foundation other than the Rock, which is Jesus Christ (see 1 Corinthians 3:11). All other foundations are unstable sand. Jesus is:

- The Source of Living Waters flowing from the Garden of Eden (Genesis 2:10)
- The Stone at the base of the stairway to Heaven (Genesis 28:18)
- The Rock in the wilderness that gushed water for the children of Israel (1 Corinthians 10:4)
- The Stone of Stumbling (Isaiah 8:14)
- The Foundation Stone (Isaiah 28:16)
- The River of Peace (Isaiah 66:12)
- The Rock upon which a wise person builds a house (Matthew 7:24-27)

- The Temple (John 2:19)
- The Chief Cornerstone (Ephesians 2:20)
- The Foundation Stone of the New Jerusalem (Revelation 21:14)
- The Source of Living Water Flowing from the Temple (Revelation 22:1-2)

Water is an absolute necessity for physical life. Likewise, *spiritual* water is a necessity for *spiritual life*. The river of peace springs up as a fountain within us, continually refreshing us with new life. We can *stay connected* with supernatural peace that flows like a river. *"Whoever drinks of the water that I shall give him will never thirst. But the water that I shall give him will become in him a **fountain of water** springing up into everlasting life"* (John 4:14).

> **Spiritual water is a necessity for spiritual life.**

This fresh, life-giving water flows continuously from Genesis to Revelation and springs up in our hearts today.

NOTES

1. "Most Americans still believe in God," *Gallup News*, June 29, 2016; http://news .gallup.com/poll/193271/americans-believe-god.aspx; accessed November 9, 2017.

2. Andrew Murray, *God's Will: Our Dwelling Place* (New Kensington, PA: Whitaker House Publishers, 1991), 11–12.

3. Ibid.

4. William Wilson, *New Wilson's Old Testament Word Studies* (Grand Rapids, MI: Kregel Publishers, 1987), 153.

5. The Garden of Eden, tabernacle of Moses, and the temple were types, or shadows, patterned after a heavenly reality. God showed Moses the heavenly tabernacle and cautioned him to build exactly like the pattern shown (see Exodus 25:8-9). Later, David gave his son, Solomon, the pattern for the temple (see 1 Chronicles 28:10-12). They were designed by God, not man, to be copies of the sanctuary of God in Heaven. T. Desmond Alexander, author of *From Eden to the New Jerusalem: An Introduction to Biblical Theology*, suggests

that Genesis "portrays the Garden of Eden as a sanctuary or temple-garden" as a "place where divinity and humanity enjoy each other's presence." Therefore, he continues, "It is appropriate that it should be a prototype for later Israelite sanctuaries. This explains why many of the decorative features of the tabernacle and temple are arboreal in nature." Even the menorah has a tree-like shape reminiscent of the Tree of Life. [T. D. Alexander, *From Eden to the New Jerusalem: An Introduction to Biblical Theology* (Grand Rapids, MI: Kregel Academic and Professional Publishing, 2009), 25.]

6. The topography of the earth has been altered considerably since the time of the creation of the world. Natural disasters and floods have occurred. Tectonic plates have shifted. Rivers have dried up and the courses of other rivers have been changed. The Bible describes what could be tectonic/volcanic activity in the destruction of Sodom and Gomorrah in Abraham's day. Much time and effort has been expended in the attempt to find the location of the Garden of Eden. Looking to the Bible for clues, we find a great deal of support for Israel as the location of Eden. God clearly considers Israel to be His Holy land (see Ezekiel 20:40). At the time of creation, Eden was His holy land. Abraham was told to sacrifice Isaac (a type of the sacrifice of Jesus) on Mount Moriah (see Genesis 22:2). Solomon built the Temple "at Jerusalem at Mount Moriah" (see 2 Chronicles 3:1). Jesus was crucified at Jerusalem. We can speculate that perhaps God sacrificed a lamb for a skin to cover Adam and Eve at the same location (see Genesis 3:21). If so, by extension, we can infer that the central point of the Garden of Eden was in the geographical region of Jerusalem. Many scholars have studied this topic extensively, and there is much biblical support for this hypothesis in numerous books on the subject. [T. D. Alexander, *From Eden to the New Jerusalem: An Introduction to Biblical Theology* (Grand Rapids, MI: Kregel Academic and Professional Publishing, 2009).]

7. In Jewish tradition, Israel was the center of the world, Jerusalem was the center of Israel, the temple was the center of Jerusalem, the Holy Place was the center of the temple, the Holy of Holies was the center of the Holy Place, and the foundation stone under the ark of the Covenant was the center of the Holy of Holies. The creation of the world was said to have begun at the site of that stone, and it was believed that the prophesied living waters would spring from it." [C. S. Keener, *The Spirit in the Gospels and Acts: Divine Purity and Power* (Peabody, MA: Hendrickson Publishers, 1997); D. Ward, "Rivers of Living Water," *Grace and Knowledge: A Journal of Judeo-Christian History*, Theology and Culture; http://graceandknowledge.faithweb.com/john7.html]; accessed May 3, 2013.

THE PRACTICALITY
OF GOD'S WILL

CHAPTER 7

PEACE IS LOVE RULING

By Jennifer

Based on what I had previously been taught, I once believed the fruit of the Spirit grew as the result of godly character. But how could I actually tell if I had any? I lived in low-grade anxiety most of the time; so much so that Dennis called me "little much afraid" when we first met, after the main character in Hannah Hurnard's book, *Hinds Feet on High Places*. Peace? It was more a mental concept than an experience for me. Joy was likewise a great puzzle. Was that like the excitement I felt about birthday parties as a child? How can we recapture feeling that as an adult? It seemed very mysterious, but I wanted it.

Needless to say, when an intriguing flyer arrived in the mail announcing an upcoming women's conference on the joy of the Lord, I registered right away. The conference turned out to be a big disappointment, however. The speakers taught what the Bible said *about* joy for the most part. One woman said she had experienced supernatural joy once, even though she was going through a rough time in her life, but didn't know how she got "it" or if it would ever happen again. Apparently no one had joy or knew how to get it! This was very discouraging.

I didn't learn anything else about joy until 1997, after Dennis and I were married. It was wonderful news to discover he had the very answers I was looking for. One of the first evenings we prayed together, he asked me to close my eyes and get in an attitude of prayer. Next, he told me to put my hand on my belly and yield my heart to Christ within. Belly? That was different. I had never connected heart and belly before, but John 7:38 (KJV) flashed in my mind: *"He that believeth on me, as the scripture hath said, out of his **belly** shall flow rivers of living water."*

Because Dennis operates in a strong gifting of discerning of spirits, he was able to bear witness to what I was feeling. As I also learned later, we emanate an anointing when we touch the presence of God. When believers are in a worship service, the atmosphere feels "worshipful" because of the anointing flowing from their hearts. An anointing also flows through us when we open our hearts toward others and allow a river of love to flow to them.

As a matter of fact, we create a carnal or spiritual emotional atmosphere around us that can influence others, for good or bad.

> [The] process in which a person or a group influences the emotions and affective behavior of another person or group through the conscious or unconscious induction of emotions is referred to as emotional contagion.... When a [sports] team is upbeat, positive, and in an overall good mood, this spirit is transferred to individual players. Results also show that when teams are happier, the athletes on the team tend to play better.... Research has found that depression in a spouse frequently leads to depression in the partner. The same holds true for roommates. In addition, children raised by depressed parents are significantly more likely to be diagnosed with depression. In fact, one family members' depression can bring down an entire family system. Other emotions, such as anxiety and fear, can have the same effect.[1]

For we are to God the pleasing aroma of Christ among those who are being saved and those who are perishing (2 Corinthians 2:15-NIV).

Because my focus was now on the Lord rather than on myself, I experienced a subtle awareness of the presence of God. It definitely felt different from anxiety! Dennis explained, "That's the *peace* of God." Then he said, "Open your heart more and go deeper." Without any real understanding of what I was doing, I "relaxed" more, which caused me to yield to God more. I felt something "effervescent" inside and I smiled. Dennis told me, "That joy bubble you're feeling, that's the joy of the Lord."

I had never heard such a simple and practical explanation of spiritual functioning so, from that time on I kept a record of all the small steps Dennis taught me. Moreover, what he was teaching me really worked. Although I had read books by many of the great men and women of God about their spiritual experiences, such as *The Practice of the Presence of God* by Brother Lawrence, their experiences seemed impossible to duplicate. Finally, I began to have a spiritual life of my own.

Now that I was able to actually experience what the Bible said, I began to research the theology that corroborated what I was learning about the heart.

HEART IN THE SCRIPTURES

OLD TESTAMENT

Only when we locate our spirit-heart correctly can we effectively *guard our heart*. Proverbs 4:23 tells us *"out of it spring the issues of life."* The heart is the center of humankind's inward life and the sphere of divine influence. Whenever the Bible talks about the heart as our innermost being, it is not referring to the chest or physical heart.

The most common word for "heart" in the Old Testament is the Hebrew word *leb* (*lev*) or *lebab* (*levav*), which is translated "heart" in this verse of Scripture. It occurs almost 600 times in the Old Testament. The term *leb* is very general, referring to many aspects of our being including our innermost being, will, inclinations, understanding, soul, memory, passions, and resolve.

> *Love the Lord your God with all your heart* [Hebrew: lev], *with all your soul, and with all your strength* (Deuteronomy 6:5).

However, other words are also used that specifically indicate that the location of the heart is in the belly. *Me`ah*, Strong's #4578, translated figuratively as "heart," literally means intestines, abdomen, belly; also stomach, womb (or for men, the seat of generation, the loins), belly, and bowels.

> *I delight to do thy will, O my God: yea, thy law is within my heart* [Hebrew: me`ah] (Psalm 40:8 KJV).

> *I am poured out like water, and all my bones are out of joint: my heart* [lev] *is like wax; it is melted in the midst of my bowels* [Hebrew: me`ah] (Psalm 22:14 KJV).

The Jews correctly regarded the gut as the seat of tender affections, particularly kindness, benevolence, and compassion, but also passion, mourning, and suffering. Another word used to refer to the heart is *beten*, literally meaning belly, abdomen, inward parts, womb, and sometimes the seat of physical hunger, but also used figuratively for innermost being or heart.

> *The words of a talebearer are as wounds, and they go down into the innermost parts of the belly* [Hebrew: beten, belly, abdomen, womb, inner man, heart] (Proverbs 18:8 KJV).

NEW TESTAMENT

In the New Testament, the heart, at our core or mid section, is the *epicenter* of our emotions, moral nature, and spiritual life—which, as in John 7:38, resides in the "belly" (*koilia* in the original Greek). *Koilia's* literal meaning is belly, abdomen, bowels, stomach, and womb. Figuratively, *koilia* refers to the innermost being or heart.

> *He that believeth on me, as the scripture hath said, out of his belly* [Greek: *koilia*, belly, abdomen, womb, inner man] *shall flow rivers of living water* (John 7:38 KJV).

Splanchnon, used nine times in the New Testament, is also translated as "heart." The literal meaning is inward parts, innards, viscera, intestines, and womb and, figuratively, compassion, affections, and the seat of the emotions.

> *For God is my record, how greatly I long after you all in the bowels* [Greek: *splanchnon*, intestines, affection, compassion, tender mercies] *of Jesus Christ* (Philippians 1:8 KJV).

The Greek word *kardia*, meaning "heart," can mean either the figurative heart or the physical heart. In the New Testament, however, *kardia* is used 159 times for our emotional and spiritual center, but is used literally in only one verse of Scripture that refers to physical death caused by fear:

> *Men's hearts* [Greek: *kardia*] *failing them from fear and the expectation of those things...coming on the earth...* (Luke 21:26).

It is important to note that our human spirit is not located in an actual physical organ of the body. Our spirit is not physical matter or energy (a form of matter) such as chemical, electrical, or thermal energy. The Bible tells us a spiritual realm exists, God is a

Spirit (see John 4:24), angels are spirits (see Hebrews 1:13-14), and we are spirit beings in a material body. We can only know and worship God by approaching Him spirit-to-Spirit. *"God is Spirit, and those who worship Him must worship in spirit and truth"* (John 4:24).

Within our heart, we find the following:

- Divine influence (Romans 2:15; Acts 15:9)
- The spirit (Proverbs 20:27; 2 Corinthians 1:22; Galatians 4:2; 1 Peter 3:4)
- The seat of grief (see John 14:1; Romans 9:2; 2 Corinthians 2:4)
- Joy (see John 16:22; Ephesians 5:19)
- The desires (see Matthew 5:28; 2 Peter 2:14)
- The affections (see Luke 24:32; Acts 21:13)
- The perceptions (see John 12:40; Ephesians 4:18)
- The understanding (see Matthew 13:15; Romans 1:21)
- The reasoning powers (see Mark 2:6; Luke 24:38)
- The imagination (see Luke 1:51)
- The conscience (see Acts 2:37; 1 John 3:20)
- The intentions (see Hebrews 4:12; 1 Peter 4:1)
- Purpose (see Acts 11:23; 2 Corinthians 9:7)
- The will (see Romans 6:17; Colossians 3:15)
- Faith (see Mark 11:23; Romans 10:10; Hebrews 3:12)

LOCATION

SEAT OF THE EMOTIONS

Most people associate heart with emotions. Our heart is our "emotional brain." We have already established that our heart is the seat of our emotions, and it resides in the belly according to the Scriptures (see Matthew 5:28; Luke 24:32; John 7:38; John 16:22; Ephesians 5:19). In modern terminology, we talk about gut hunches, gut feelings, or gut reactions. Often people are told to "go with their gut" when making decisions. This means it generally works out better to listen to the heart in addition to the head, rather than the head alone. Our choices are usually wiser when they're based on more than mental reasoning alone.

> *Guard your heart above all else, for it determines the course of your life* (Proverbs 4:23 NLT).

Have you heard the old saying, "You can miss heaven by eighteen inches"? That is the distance between your head and physical heart, located in your chest. That saying refers to head versus heart Christianity. It is possible to have intellectual knowledge but no heart knowledge. But according to the Bible, our heart is actually located a little more than 18 inches from our heads. The location of our emotional heart is in the belly, out of which love and compassion flow.

> *Joseph made haste; for his bowels did yearn upon his brother: and he sought where to weep; and he entered into his chamber, and wept there* (Genesis 43:30 KJV).

> *Mine eyes do fail with tears, my bowels are troubled…* (Lamentations 2:11 KJV).

> *For God is my record, how greatly I long after you all in the bowels* [affection] *of Jesus Christ* (Philippians 1:8 KJV).

Not only do love and compassion flow from there, but the Bible says the wounds of the heart are also located in the belly:

"The words of a talebearer are as wounds, and they go down into the innermost parts of the belly" (Proverbs 18:8 KJV). They take on a life of their own and will resurface every time someone or something pushes that "button." Negative emotions remain lodged in the heart until they are dislodged by forgiveness. Emotions don't die; we just bury them alive!

THOUGHTS

Everyone seems to know where thoughts are located—in the head. There's no confusion on that one. Thoughts are formed in the brain by recalling information stored in our memory, and by processing that information, we are applying knowledge to make decisions and solve problems. The conscious mind is aware of only a fraction of brain activity at any given time. But our entire life story, every minute detail, is actually stored away in our nonconscious mind.

We have all forgotten far more than we will ever remember. The truth is that when someone describes a crisis after-the-fact, they often say, "I saw my whole life pass before my eyes." That's because long-forgotten memories were retrieved and brought into conscious awareness once again.

Every thought we have has a corresponding emotion attached to it. Feeling nostalgic when we smell something connected with a pleasant childhood memory exemplifies this well. Something like freshly baked cookies or the evergreen smell of Christmas can bring back a flood of memories and emotions attached to those memories. This is true of both positive and negative emotions.

Memories are stored as *feeling-thought* combinations.[2] That's why some memories still make us feel sad and others stir up happy feelings deep within. The thoughts that cause us the most trouble, of course, are those connected to negative emotions.

WILL

The Bible tells us that the center of choice and volition is in the heart. And we have already established that our Bible heart is in our belly. In the Old Testament, the Hebrew word for "reins" is sometimes used for the will. The literal translation for "reins" is kidneys, which locates the seat of our volition in the gut. Jeremiah said: *"I the Lord search the heart, I try the reins* [kidneys]*, even to give every man according to his ways* [choices]*..."* (Jeremiah 17:10 KJV).

Exerting our own willpower creates stress within our body. Willpower is the force of our own will trying to control our person, other people, or the circumstances of life. As soon as we feel tense or stressed, stress hormones are released throughout our body, and our muscles contract. Whenever we face a perceived threat, our entire body reacts by going into self-protection mode. But we feel it first in the gut.

If we pay attention the next time a minor inconvenience occurs, we'll notice that our muscles tighten in our gut. Although we might not realize it at the moment, we can learn to catch ourselves at this early stage and let it go from the gut. However, if we continue in stress, our muscular tension is likely to increase and spread to our back, shoulders, and neck.

DOOR OF THE HEART

At the time of salvation, we opened the door of our heart to Jesus and invited Him in. *"Look! I stand at the door and knock. If you hear my voice and open the door, I will come in..."* (Revelation 3:20 NLT). Our will opens and shuts the door of our heart.

When we are suspicious about someone's motives, we can close our heart to that person. Our heart says, "No, I will not be vulnerable to that person." However, when we close the door of our heart with willpower and put up a wall, it doesn't actually protect us.

That wall is a product of fear, so the *"fiery darts"* of the enemy can go right through it (Ephesians 6:16). Moreover, when we close the door of our heart, our control shuts the door on Jesus, too.

A better way to handle such situations would be to yield even more to Christ within and let peace be our guard. It might make you feel vulnerable at first, but when peace is ruling, Jesus Himself is protecting you.

How about stress? When we begin to feel tension in our gut, it's a sign that our willpower has been engaged. When we trust in God's help, we open the *door of our heart* to Him, and automatically relax, or yield control. We can't be stressed and trust God at the same time.

PRACTICE
EXPERIENCING PEACE IN PRAYER

Sit down in a quiet room and close your eyes. Place your hand on your belly. Relax and yield to Christ in you. Focus on your heart and notice a gentle sense of peace. We become more aware of the Lord when we pay attention to Him.

Honor God by acknowledging the fact that His Spirit is within you.

Spend a few minutes waiting in the presence of God. Often, as we become more relaxed, our awareness of peace increases.

Note: *We shouldn't ever attempt to make our mind go "blank," but simply focus on Christ within and be aware that He is with us. Focus is the opposite of blank.*

TERMINOLOGY

As we attempted to explain subjective experiences, we coined some new terminology. For that reason, we have included a short explanation of some terms.

BIBLE HEART

In the Old Testament and New Testament alike, Hebrew and Greek words describing the *belly* or *bowels* are regularly translated "heart" in our English versions. Our heart is described as residing in "the depths" of our being, or as David said, in the "innermost being" and "hidden part" of us (see Psalm 51:6). Our human spirit fills us from head to toe but our heart is the epicenter of spiritual and emotion activity.

To differentiate between the physical heart and our heart which the Bible calls our inner being, we use the term *Bible heart*. Only when we locate our spirit-heart correctly can we effectively *guard our heart*. Proverbs 4:23 tells us that out of our heart *"spring the issues of life."*

DROP DOWN

The term *drop down* was a phrase Dennis used when he reminded me to stop thinking so much and focus on Christ within. As soon as we drop down to our spirit and include the Lord, we should feel a gentle awareness that He is with us. We have shifted our focus from our head to our heart. We then experience the peace of His presence. It is much the same as driving a car with a passenger in the back seat. You may not be able to see them, but you know they are there.

Peace can seem very gentle and subtle. Don't expect lightning bolts or euphoria. Small children may use the word *good* to describe peace. Even if you only feel a mild sense of well-being, as long as you are aware of Christ within, you are experiencing the peace of His presence. The more we yield, the more peace we feel.

BUCKET MAN

A number of years ago we made a "bucket man" poster as a visual aid for Sunday school based on the concept of dropping down.

When we drop down to our spirit, we tap into the living waters in our heart. *"The water that I shall give…will become…a fountain of water springing up into everlasting life"* (John 4:14). A picture of a crank with rope wrapped around it with a hole in the middle is placed over "bucket man's" head. A piece of string is threaded through the hole and tied to a cardboard bucket. When the bucket goes down, blue cardboard "water" is Velcroed to the bucket to represent living water. When the bucket goes up to bucket man's head, the water is removed.

Focus is like a spiritual "bucket." When we open the door of our heart to God, our bucket drops down to the fountain springing up in our heart. When we focus on our thoughts, we pull the bucket back up to our head. One young child commented, "There's no living water in our head!" The children love the bucket man illustration, but it helps adults catch on as well. We often say, "Your bucket is up," or "Drop your bucket down."

> *Counsel in the heart of man is like water in a deep well, but a man of understanding draws it out* (Proverbs 20:5 AMPC).

NOTES

1. Sherri Bourg Carter, "Emotions Are Contagious: Choose Your Companions Wisely," *Psychology Today*, October 20, 2012; https://www.psychologytoday.com/blog/high-octane-women/201210/emotions-are-contagious-choose-your-company-wisely; accessed June 22, 2017.

2. Michael D. Gershon, *The Second Brain: A Groundbreaking New Understanding of Nervous Disorders of the Stomach and Intestine* (New York, NY: HarperCollins, 1999).

CHAPTER 8

PEACE AND FORGIVENESS

By Jen

One of the most powerful lessons a believer can learn is how to *yield* their will to God's will. Yielding instantly connects us to Christ within. When we are connected to Him, we experience the peace of His presence. When we have peace, we are trusting God. When we're at peace, we're in the flow of God's will! Wherever the Lord moves, we move with Him…automatically.

Now that I knew how to *tap into* peace, I faced a new challenge—*living* in peace. It was one thing to "visit" peace, but it took much practice for me to live there. For most of the first year of our marriage, I felt like a yoyo—up and down all the time. Fortunately, both Dennis and the Lord reminded me to drop down to peace whenever I became upset or anxious. Eventually, peace became my lifestyle. When we live in peace, we abide in His life: *"I am the vine, you are the branches. He who abides in Me, and I in him, bears much fruit; for without Me you can do nothing"* (John 15:5). As we practice abiding, the Lord continually guides us and our lives become fruitful.

Yielding connects us to Christ within.

If we are truly trusting God, our heart is at peace. We rest in Him rather than trying to control our own life. Proverbs 3:5-6 explains how to stay in the flow. *"Trust in the Lord with all your heart, and lean not on your own understanding; in all your ways acknowledge Him, and He shall direct your paths."* The word *acknowledge* (Hebrew *yada'*) is of great significance in this passage of Scripture:

> [T]he highest level of *yada'* is in "direct intimate contact." This refers to life-giving intimacy, as in marriage. Applied to a spiritual context, it suggests an intimacy with God... that conceives and births blessings and victories. Joined to our...[Proverbs text], we might conclude that, if in all our "days" we maintain *yada'* (direct intimate contact with God), God promises to direct our paths toward fruitful, life-begetting endeavors.[1]

TWO SPIRITUAL KINGDOMS

Only two spiritual kingdoms exist: God's Kingdom and the enemy's kingdom. Emotions reveal which kingdom we've tapped into. Emotions are signals that reveal our spiritual condition. The fruit of the Spirit is evidence that Jesus is ruling: *"Let the peace of God rule"* (Colossians 3:15). Our emotions were created to be conduits, or "pipes," for the fruit of the Spirit. When Adam and Eve lived in the Garden of Eden before sin entered the picture, they had perfect harmony with God and one another. The only emotions they felt were God's emotions. We experience the love of God as the fruit of the Spirit—one fruit, multiple functions (see Galatians 5:22-23).

Emotions were created for the fruit of the Spirit.

- Joy is love rejoicing (we find deep pleasure in God's presence).

- Peace is love ruling (we are under the lordship of Jesus).

- Patience is love enduring (we are willing to wait for God's timing).

- Kindness is love giving (we serve others with mercy).

- Goodness is love motivating (our heart is moved by love and holiness).

- Faith is love trusting (we can believe God and others can believe us).

- Gentleness is love esteeming (we *"esteem others better"* than ourselves, see Philippians 2:3).

- Self-control is love restraining (we are *"kept by the power of God,"* 1 Peter 1:5).

As soon as sin fractured the harmony of the Garden, Adam and Eve felt negative emotions for the first time. In a few short passages of Scripture, we see that they experienced hurt, fear, anger, guilt, and shame—emotions from the pit of hell. Toxic emotions let us know we have made a detour into enemy territory. The loss of peace lets us know immediately that we have an internal issue to deal with or we need to make a course correction.

In the book of Colossians, we find an often ignored but very powerful key: *"As you...have received Christ...so walk in Him"* (Colossians 2:6). How do we receive Jesus as our Savior? We *open* the door of our heart to Jesus, receive *forgiveness* instantly as a free

"As you received Christ, so walk."

gift, and experience peace with God, the *fruit* of the Spirit: *open-forgiveness-fruit*.

We live the Christian life the same way. We keep our heart *open* to God by living with a yielded will (see Revelation 3:20). Any negative emotions let us know we have disconnected. We can then apply *forgiveness* to remove the toxic emotion separating us from God's presence (see 1 John 1:7). The *fruit* of the Spirit is evidence that we have reconnected with the Lord (see Colossians 3:15; Philippians 4:9): *open-forgiveness-fruit*.

DESTINY DESTROYERS

What happens when we *don't* apply forgiveness and remove negative emotions? Buried toxic emotions cause repetitive cycles of trouble. They are like seeds that spring up and produce harvests of poisonous weeds. Toxic emotions themselves are not sin. However, we commit the sin of unforgiveness when we allow them to remain in our heart.

When negative emotions planted in our heart are triggered by people or circumstances in our life, we overreact, become immobilized, or act impulsively. They set us up *Toxic emotions stunt our emotional growth.* for recurring cycles of trouble. By stunting our emotional growth, they also trap us in childish attitudes and behaviors. In addition, they distort our perception so we can't see people and life clearly. Because of hidden negative emotions, we see life through a distorted lens, miss opportunities, and harm relationships. The main destiny destroyers lurk within our own heart.

When we have unresolved issues, our heart has hidden emotional "land mines." They manifest every time the events of life trigger them. In the natural, land mines explode only once.

Toxic emotions, on the other hand, explode repeatedly until they are removed by forgiveness. Emotions don't die; they get buried alive!

Right after Dennis and I were married, he prayed with me on a regular basis for approximately two months, using the principles found in this book. It changed my life forever. Although I once felt "under attack" on a regular basis, after I let the Lord cleanse my heart, skirmishes with the enemy became rare. If you have been plagued by what seems to be "spiritual warfare" on a regular basis, we suggest you spend time with the Lord and allow Him to remove emotional land mines. Most of the roots are hidden or forgotten in the nonconscious part of our being. Our conscious mind is like a bucket of sand, but our nonconscious is like the rest of the sand on the whole beach. It is alarming to realize that those things we have *forgotten* can still control our life and cause us trouble!

Only God knows our whole heart. That's why David asked God to search his heart for *hidden* issues so they wouldn't control him. *"How can I know all the sins lurking in my heart? Cleanse me from these hidden faults. ...Don't let them control me"* (Psalm 19:12-13 NLT).

David prayed, *"Search me, O God, and know my heart; try me and know my anxious thoughts; and see if there be any hurtful way in me, and lead me in the everlasting way"* (Psalm 139:23-24 NASB). Notice that David speaks of thoughts that are anxious and ways that are hurtful. This clear interweaving of our heart, tying together emotional thoughts and our emotional choices, is corroborated by modern science.

"Search me, O God!"

The evidence has been piling up throughout history, and now neuroscientists have proved it's true: The brain's wiring emphatically relies on emotion over intellect in decision-making…. In fact, people who lack emotions because of brain injuries often have difficulty making decisions at all…. The brain stores emotional memories of past decisions, and those are what drive people's choices in life…. [Neuroscientist Antonio Damasio] says: "What makes you and me 'rational' is not suppressing our emotions, but tempering them in a positive way."[2]

FORGIVENESS RELEASES US

Jesus already paid the penalty for our sin of unforgiveness. Forgiveness releases us and others to God so that He can work in our lives. Forgiveness sets us free. In other words, when we allow Christ to forgive through us, we cease to sit in the place of judgment: we release ourselves and others into God's hands.

Forgiveness is the secret for living in peace as a lifestyle. It removes hidden wounds and empowers you to restore and maintain your peace whenever issues arise in everyday living. It can change everything in your life. It's not just for salvation, major betrayals and wounds, or for the confessional. If you're like most people, you live with intermittent, if not constant, anxiety, worry, or annoyance. Minor offenses and emotional setbacks—with your spouse, children, coworkers, or strangers—are ongoing struggles.

Forgiveness is way to maintain a heart connection with Christ. The regular practice of forgiveness keeps us in the river of God's will.

FORGIVENESS DEFINED

Many of us have been taught a wrong view of forgiveness. We somehow equate it with being a doormat or excusing a person of his/her responsibility in a situation. However, when we forgive, we are not pardoning in the sense of removing any consequences for one's sin or absolving another's sin. We are not pretending to forget about what happened or reconciling with a person when boundaries still need to be established. We are not releasing them from responsibility.

But what we *are* doing is canceling the debt that was committed against us. We are ceasing to sit in the place of judgment and releasing perpetrators to God.

Forgiveness is not the same as reconciliation. We are required to forgive as freely as Jesus forgave those who crucified Him. However, reconciliation requires genuine repentance on the part of the offender as well as a change in behavior. The right to reconciliation must be earned because restored relationship requires restored trust.

CHRIST THE FORGIVER

Based on our own observations over the years, most believers don't know how to forgive properly, effectively, and deliberately so that lingering negative emotions are healed permanently. Even if some Christians occasionally succeed at forgiving and find emotional freedom, they don't know exactly what they did or how they did it—and they can't teach forgiveness to others.

We may say we forgive someone who has offended us—but forgiveness is not just saying the right words. We may pray fervently with tears—but forgiveness is not just an emotional release. We may even determine to forgive by making a quality decision—but forgiveness is not an act of exerting our own will. Forgiveness is much more than mere mental assent, feeling sorry for oneself, or doing a good deed. It is a supernatural encounter with Christ the

Forgiver. We forgive by the grace of God. Christ Himself does the forgiving through us. The Forgiver in us does all the work. And everything He does is easy for Him!

Although forgiving others is commanded by the Word of God, many of us still harbor small resentments throughout the day. Forgiveness is not optional. If we don't forgive others, God won't forgive us: *"if you refuse to forgive others, your Father will not forgive your sins"* (Matthew 6:15 NLT). That doesn't mean that we are condemned if we don't forgive. It only means that we have to live with the torment of our own unforgiveness.

Emotions are not sin. Harboring negative emotions in our heart through unforgiveness is sinful, however. Jesus already paid the penalty for sin and gave us the gift of forgiveness. When we allow Christ to forgive through us, we release ourselves and others into God's hands. At the time of salvation, you didn't have to work for forgiveness or beg God for it. You received it with childlike faith. You simply opened the door of your heart and received instantaneous forgiveness as a free gift.

Experiencing forgiveness in our daily lives follows exactly the same course: we call on a Person who answers immediately and cleanses us. When we received Christ as our Lord and Savior, we opened our heart to Him and instantly experienced salvation, which was accompanied by peace or joy. And so it is with encountering Christ the Forgiver: He *instantly* replaces pain with His peace—with no process required.

Christ forgives through us.

WHO TO FORGIVE

Forgiveness goes in three directions: toward God, self, and others. Sometimes we need to forgive in two or more directions. If in doubt, forgive. You can't love or forgive too much!

1. *God.* God didn't do anything wrong, but people get angry at Him anyway. Sometimes people feel hurt that God didn't do what they wanted Him to do, or become angry that God didn't *stop* something from happening. Forgiving God gets *your* heart right by releasing your judgments toward Him.

2. *Self.* If you are angry, disappointed with, or ashamed of yourself, you need to receive forgiveness for judging yourself so harshly. Frequently people are much harder on themselves than other people!

3. *Others.* Release forgiveness to other people. It sets *you* free!

PRACTICE

PRAYER STEPS

1. **FIRST.** *First thing that comes to mind.* Who or what is the first person or situation that comes to mind—in an image or memory?

2. **FEEL.** *Feel the feeling.* Allow yourself to feel. What is the emotion you feel in your gut?

3. **FORGIVE.** *Let forgiveness flow.* Yield to Christ the Forgiver within and allow a river of forgiveness to flow from the belly until the emotion changes to peace.

4. **FACT.** *Replace a lie with God's truth.* After forgiving and getting peace, if there is a lie, renounce the lie out loud. Next, ask the Lord for the truth (scriptural fact) and receive it.

5. **FILL.** *Fill emotional holes.* (1) Forgive first until you get peace. (2) Release demands on people to give you what you need. (3) Receive filling from Christ within.

Note: Most emotional healings require ONLY the first three steps: **First-Feel-Forgive**.

IMPORTANT KEYS FOR PRAYER

- Christ is the Forgiver, so forgiveness works every time!
- Forgiveness is instant, not a process.
- There is no "big or little." It is all easy for Jesus!
- Sequence is important, so always go in God's order.
- Pray through one thing at a time until you get peace.

Forgiveness is the answer for dealing with conflict and offenses in the moment as well as getting rid of the baggage of the past. God graciously cleans up a lot of things in a person's life at the time of salvation, and some ways of thinking, feeling, and motivation change immediately. However, we don't know how much was removed and what remains.

> *I acknowledged my sin to You, and my iniquity I did not hide. I said,* **I will confess my transgressions to the Lord [continually unfolding the past till all is told]**—*then You [instantly] forgave me the guilt and iniquity of my sin* (Psalm 32:5 AMPC).

Becoming healed, whole, and Christlike is a process of growth that requires heart transformation and obedience. Nobody has dealt with every single issue past and present. Therefore, let God search your heart on a regular basis so He can reveal attitudes that need adjustment and suppressed negative emotions that require cleansing.

> *[L]et's make a clean break with everything that defiles or distracts us, both within and without. Let's make our entire lives fit and holy temples for the worship of God"* (2 Corinthians 7:1 MSG).

NOTES

1. Jack W. Hayford (Editor), *Spirit-Filled Life Bible* (Nashville, TN: Thomas Nelson, Inc., 1991), 888–889.

2. Dan Vergano, "Emotions Rule the Brain's Decisions," *USA Today: Science and Space*, August 6, 2006; http://usatoday30.usatoday.com/tech/science/discoveries/2006-08-06-brain-study_x.htm; accessed June 22, 2012.

CHAPTER 9

PURSUING GOD IN PRAYER

By Dennis

You will seek Me and find Me, when you search for Me with all your heart.—Jeremiah 29:13

Although we can learn about God by reading the Bible, listening to sermons, and other forms of study, we can come to *know* Him only by spending time in His presence. The most important principle in discovering God's will is seeking God Himself. When I was a new believer in my twenties, prayer for me was being with a Person rather than just saying prayers. As soon as I closed my eyes to pray, I felt the presence of God. (Believers almost automatically drop down to their spirit and open their heart to God when they focus on Him in prayer.)

There is nothing we can do that is more important than spending time with God. This is the only way we can really get to know anybody, and that includes God. Spending time in prayer is a vital element of spiritual growth. Mental knowledge is good, but only heart knowledge produces intimacy. And without intimacy, our Christianity isn't worth much.

We can only know God by spending time in His presence.

As a young Catholic at the time I was saved, I knew little about prayer and how other people prayed but, when I closed my eyes in prayer, I *felt* the supernatural peace of God. I had always been somewhat hyperactive, so peace of any kind was a new experience for me, much less the gift of supernatural peace Jesus gives to believers (see John 14:27).

I became acclimated to "touching" His peace and living in that atmosphere. Whenever something interrupted this peace (such as a negative emotion), I wanted to return as quickly as possible. Because peace is a gift given to believers by Jesus Himself, I understood that it's always available. All disruptions, I learned, were caused by me breaking my connection with Him.

My guiding Scripture verse was Philippians 3:10 from the Amplified translation of the Bible, *"that I may know Him."* Years later I began to read Protestant books on prayer, and was confused because there was so much talking

"That I may know Him!"   involved. Convinced that my first approach was so much more satisfying, that settled the question for me. Later, I called this *Simple Prayer*—prayer of simple devotion to Jesus (see 2 Corinthians 11:3).

SIMPLE PRAYER

Simple Prayer is prayer focused on loving God and enjoying His presence. It is based in the simplicity of a life-giving relationship with the Lord. We spend time with Him and He imparts life to us. Paul cautions us to avoid being *"led astray from the **simplicity** and purity of devotion to Christ"* (see 2 Corinthians 11:2-4 NASB).

Come into the presence of the Lord *expecting* to meet with Him spirit-to-Spirit. Present your time as an offering to Him. Offer yourself to Him and yield your will. Drop down to your spirit and open the door to your heart to welcome His Spirit. Seek God for Himself alone, and make relationship with Him your top priority! Rather than praying for your

Time spent with God is the soil in which intimacy grows.

needs to be met or interceding on behalf of others, focus on the Lord first. Time spent in communion with God is the good soil in which intimacy grows.

PRACTICE

HOW TO HEAR GOD IN PRAYER

Become more sensitive to the nuances of the Spirit in touch by paying attention to the atmosphere and letting God birth revelation in your heart.

1. ***Atmosphere.*** *Focus on the presence of Christ within. Wait before the Lord and pay attention to distinctive differences. Allow God time to reveal Himself to you by waiting. What aspect of the Lord's nature is He revealing to you?*

2. ***Descriptive words to describe the atmosphere.*** *Don't try to think. Allow words to come spontaneously, such as newness, refreshing, effervescence, and so forth.*

3. ***Pictures that corroborate the atmosphere and words.*** *What pictures come to mind such as a fountain, an underground river, or a waterfall.*

4. ***Scriptures that come to mind.*** *Stay in prayer and pay attention to scripture verses that are quickened that corroborate the atmosphere, words, and pictures.*

5. ***Receive, absorb, drink in.*** *Don't just think about what the Lord is revealing. From down in the belly, absorb, drink in, the anointing.*

6. ***Cherish, live, and proclaim.*** *Value what the Lord reveals to you by receiving it into your heart, making it part of your life, and proclaim it by writing it in your journal and sharing it with others.*

JESUS IS LORD

Many believers say they love God, but they equally love their family, friends, entertainment, vacations, and material possessions. The Lord calls that *"scattered charms"* and rebuked the children of Israel for their idolatry (see Jeremiah 3:13). When we put God in first place, He promises to meet our needs:

> *…Steep your life in God-reality, God-initiative, God-provisions. Don't worry about missing out. You'll find all your everyday human concerns will be met* (Matthew 6:33 MSG).

Three key elements of prayer are honor, awareness, and time. First, honor God as a real Person who is right there with you. Next, as you sense the presence of God, pay attention to the atmosphere and spiritual impressions. Cultivate an awareness of His presence more than focusing on what you see and hear. Finally, spend enough time to become comfortably still in God's presence. If something comes to mind that you need to do later, just make a note of it and continue in prayer.

INTIMACY AND GUIDANCE

After developing a prayer life, the next element necessary for spiritual growth is learning to live under the lordship of Jesus. Many believers know Jesus as Savior—but only those who are obedient know Him as Lord. We know Jesus as Lord when He rules our daily life as we walk in union with Him—*abiding* in Him (see John 15:5).

> *Those who accept my commandments and obey them are the ones who love me. And because they love me, my Father will love them. And I will love them and reveal myself to each of them* (John 14:21 NLT).

Jesus tells us, *"Seek first the kingdom of God and His righteousness"* (Matthew 6:33). The meaning of these words is clear. We should seek the things of God above all else. In other words, diligently pursue your relationship with God and do what He wants you to do.

By learning the nuances of the presence of God, we become attuned to the guidance of the Spirit. When we practice a lifestyle of peace, we become sensitive to both the promptings and checks of the Lord. The Lord speaks to our heart not our head. Even in the natural, following the heart is usually wiser than relying upon logic alone. As we enjoy intimacy with the Lord, He will guide our steps. When we truly want the will of God for our life and stay in communion with Him, God will put *His* desires in our heart. *"Delight yourself in the Lord and He will give you the desires of your heart"* (Psalm 37:4). If we delight in God, we want His will more than getting our own way.

> *When we put God in first place, He meets our needs.*

To wholeheartedly pursue the will of God, we must:

1. Choose God's will over our own.

2. Trust God and take small steps of obedience.

3. Learn patience by waiting for God's timing.

MAKING DECISIONS

When making decisions, following the peace of God is essential. Decisions made when we're afraid or angry guarantee a bad outcome. Even if a decision would have been a good one, our timing will be wrong. Peace is the key for receiving guidance from the Lord.

> *Peace is the key for receiving guidance.*

When making decisions, be neutral about your options. In other words, let go of your preferences and be comfortable letting God decide. Then, in an attitude of prayer, present each possibility before the Lord one at a time. Peace in your gut indicates "yes," while an uncomfortable feeling means "no." If the presence of God increases more on one option than the other, that is also a "yes." If you can't make a distinction, the timing may be wrong or God has another option that hasn't occurred to you. Married couples should pray until both get a green light or red light. If one gets a "yes" and the other a "no," keep praying until you come to agreement.

> *Let the peace (soul harmony which comes) from Christ rule (act as umpire continually) in your hearts...* (Colossians 3:15 AMPC).

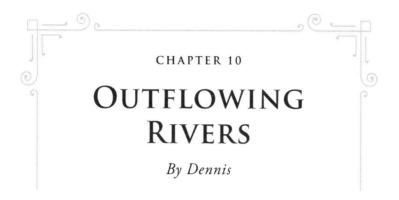

CHAPTER 10

OUTFLOWING RIVERS

By Dennis

We not only tap into peace in our heart, but rivers of living water flow from our heart. Jesus tells us that out of our belly will *"flow rivers of living water"* (John 7:38). Our human spirit functions with the Holy Spirit in five different ways as we live in the Spirit: *receiving, forgiving, loving, releasing, and resisting.*

Rivers of living water flow from our heart.

These five functions are foundational in our spiritual life. If we become proficient in utilizing these functions, we are equipped for a walk in the Spirit.

RECEIVING

The first loving function of the human spirit the Lord taught me was receiving. Opening the heart and yielding to the presence of Christ within is the way we draw in spiritual nourishment, receive impartation, and perceive revelation. We receive by absorbing, drinking in—drawing into our spirit. All spiritual substance we have received can be ministered to others.

When we read Scriptures like 1 John 3:1—*"Behold what manner of love the Father has bestowed on us, that we should be called children of God! Therefore the world does not know us, because it did not know Him.*"—how do we *receive* that Scripture? Rather than just thinking about a verse of Scripture, yield to it in your heart and allow it to become planted.

Believers sometimes close their eyes and receive the content and the anointing on a message as well as listening to the words of a sermon. What are they doing? They are drinking it into their heart rather than listening for information alone.

FORGIVING

The second function of the human spirit is forgiving. Forgiveness provides cleansing for our heart and sets us free from negative emotions. Anytime we lose our peace, forgiveness will restore our peace. Negative emotions create barriers in our heart that separate us from God and others. God conveys us into His Kingdom when we are saved. Any area with a negative emotion is back under enemy control. Forgiveness always transports us back into God's territory.

> *He* [God] *has delivered us from the power of darkness and conveyed us into the kingdom of the Son of His love, in whom we have redemption through His blood, the forgiveness of sins* (Colossians 1:13-14).

When we begin to practice connecting with Christ through dropping down, we will sometimes experience interruptions in our connection. If we feel any negative emotion, we have lost our peace. When we lose our peace, we can no longer feel the presence of God. But don't be worried. The antidote for any toxic emotion is forgiveness and/or release. Occasionally we simply need to release a person or situation into the hands of God and let go of our control.

If the interruption was just a mere temptation that briefly distracted us, causing us to lose a sense of God's presence, we can simply release it from the gut and we'll instantly get our peace back. For example, if your spouse forgot to pick up the dry cleaning and you feel irritated, you can release it to God right away and get your peace back immediately. If you get angry and dwell on it for even a few minutes, you need to release forgiveness.

Forgiveness is not a principle but an encounter with the Prince of Peace Himself, Christ the Forgiver within. Christ is the One who forgives and He dwells within us. When we need to extend or receive forgiveness, we simply allow Him to go to any toxic emotion in our heart and wash it away.

> *Forgiveness is an encounter with Christ the Forgiver.*

The internal evidence that forgiveness has taken place is that the negative emotion changes to peace. Forgiveness is not complete if we still feel the unpleasant emotion. That is how we know we did it right. If in doubt, we only need to close our eyes and think of the person or event that was associated with the negative emotion. If we have peace where there was once pain, we did it right. If hurt, fear, lust, anger, guilt or shame is still there, we need to forgive.

In watching Dennis minister, it didn't take too long for me (Jen) to see that the Holy Spirit works according to certain patterns and similarities. I noticed first of all that God is quite capable of bringing to mind what need He wants to address as well as the order or sequence He chooses. As I observed, I noticed that Dennis always followed the lead of the Holy Spirit, so when I made notes of the steps of ministry, I simply wrote down how the Holy Spirit was working. Neither Dennis nor I "came up with a method." We simply documented how God works. After all, the Holy Spirit is the minister. Our only job is to allow Him to do the work and be His facilitators, assisting those to whom He is ministering.

Remember, God will always save a person who wants to be saved. In the same way, the Lord is always present to forgive. He is always present to sanctify a heart presented to Him. Sanctification includes the removal of pain, anger, and fear in our heart through forgiveness.

The Lord is always present to forgive.

"I have been crucified with Christ; it is no longer I who live, but Christ lives in me" (Galatians 2:20). If I no longer live, but Christ lives in me, then it is no longer I who love, but Christ who loves through me. This also suggests that it is no longer I who forgive, but Christ who forgives through me.

PRACTICE

STEPS OF FORGIVENESS

Prayer. Get in an attitude of prayer. Close your eyes and drop down.

First. First person or situation. Who or what is the first person or situation God brings to mind—in an image or memory?

Feel. Feel the feeling. What is the emotion you feel in your gut?

Forgive. Yield your will and let Christ the Forgiver flow out toward the person, yourself, or God. You don't forgive a situation; you release it. If a situation came to mind such as a heavy workload at work, release it into the hands of God from the gut.

Forgiveness can flow to others, ourselves, or to God. Let a river of forgiveness flow to others, drink forgiveness in for yourself (just like when you got saved), and let forgiveness flow out to God. (God didn't do anything wrong, but we must forgive Him when we are angry at Him to set ourselves free.)

Note: Occasionally, you may need one or two additional steps of Fact and Fill in perhaps one out of every 30 or 40 emotional healings.

> **Fact.** *Most emotional wounds do not have a lie attached. Occasionally a lie may be believed at the time of an emotional wounding and become a mental stronghold. Let forgiveness flow first until you have peace, then, renounce the lie out loud. Ask the Holy Spirit for the truth (fact) and allow it to be written on your heart. Receive it and drink it in.*
>
> **Fill.** *Then, if there was an emotional need that wasn't met, such as love or attention, forgive first, then release demands on people, and receive filling from the Holy Spirit.*

LOVING

The third function of the human spirit is loving intercession. We can picture somebody and then, down low, release a river of love and allow it to flow from our heart to the person. We don't need words to release supernatural love to someone. However, when we add words, they will carry an anointing of love. Loving intercession is an experience happening within us and flowing outward from our heart. We sow good deeds or finances the same way. We release love from our heart while we are sowing. That way what we sow is conveyed from the realm of the natural into the Kingdom of God. Love is released from our heart through:

- *Loving intercession.* *"Therefore I exhort first of all that supplications, prayers, intercessions, and giving of thanks be made for all men"* (1 Timothy 2:1).

- *Worship.* *"[W]orship God in the Spirit, rejoice in Christ Jesus, and have no confidence in the flesh"* (Philippians 3:3).

- *Compassion for miracles.* *"And when Jesus went out He saw a great multitude; and He was moved with compassion for them, and healed their sick"* (Matthew 14:14).

- *Righteousness (obedience motivated by the love of God).*
  "Let your light so shine before men, that they may see your good works and glorify your Father in heaven" (Matthew 5:16).

PRACTICE

LOVING

Loving Intercession: Without words, yield to Christ within and let a river of loving intercession flow out to any person who comes to mind.

Worship: Without words, release a river of worship to flow toward God.

Compassion: Allow a river of compassion to flow to someone in need of a miracle.

Righteous Deeds: Allow the Lord to show you something He wants you to do. When you do it, allow a river of anointing to flow.

RELEASING

The fourth loving function is releasing from our belly, and it is similar to forgiveness. When we release, we're not forgiving but letting go. Say that we have a workload piled up on our desk and we feel anxious about it. When we release something (or someone) into the hands of God, anxiety changes to peace. Why? It is because we have entrusted it to God, so we are no longer carrying the burden ourselves. Jesus invites us to this place of rest:

> *Come to Me, all you who labor and are heavy laden, and I will give you rest. Take My yoke upon you and learn from Me, for I am gentle and lowly in heart, and you will find rest for your souls. For My yoke is easy and My burden is light* (Matthew 11:28-30).

When we release from our heart, we give people and circumstances to God. It is like an internal jubilee takes place. We place our problems into the hands of a loving and capable God who is able to do what He knows is best. If we release our children into His hands, He watches over them and works in their lives. We are not being irresponsible; we are simply releasing into the realm of the Kingdom. When we hang on to things, our willpower actually hinders God from working.

PRACTICE

RELEASING

Close your eyes in prayer. Put your hand on your belly. Picture anything you are holding onto with willpower: person, place, thing, or situation.

Feel. *Feel the feeling in your gut. It could be anxiety, pressure, or fear. Notice that you feel tense, not relaxed.*

Release. *Release the person, place, thing, or situation into the hands of Jesus by allowing a river of release to flow out until you feel peace.*

RESISTING

The fifth loving function of the human spirit is resisting. There is a right way to resist and a wrong way. For example, the wrong way to resist, and many believers do this regularly, is to see someone we don't want to talk to so we close the door of our heart. We become tense in our gut, which means we have put up a wall with our will. Even though we might be able to put on a smile and talk to them, inwardly we are protecting ourselves.

There is a proper way to resist. God has given us the ability to resist any negative atmosphere around us and guard our hearts with His peace. We can feel the atmosphere around us but experience peace in our heart. We bear witness to outside pressure but don't take it in.

In a hostile environment or when you are in the presence of an angry person, drop down and let the peace of God guard your heart and your mind. Remember, we don't open our heart to the person; we open our heart to Christ in us. That way Jesus "stands" between us and any person who might confront us. Because Jesus is guarding us, we can resist attacks from both flesh and spirit. The enemy can't touch the fruit of the Spirit.

Both God and the devil want our will. Why is our will so important? God's will is a flow of divine purpose. In Heaven, God's will is always perfectly expressed. He wants His will done on earth through yielded vessels. When we yield our will to God's will, we allow Heaven to be released on earth through us.

Both God and the devil want our will so they can express their *nature* through us. God's nature is love, and He wants to bring redemption to humankind. The devil's nature is fear and hate, and he wants to bring destruction and death to us. God has a divine plan for earth and He seeks those who will co-labor with Him. The devil has an evil plan for earth and he ensnares people to cooperate with him (see John 10:9-10).

The enemy can't touch the fruit of the Spirit.

God wants to work in and through His people on earth. He wants to connect with us, own us, and express His nature through us. When we live a yielded life, we are transformed more and more into the image of Christ. Peter reminds us:

> But you are a chosen race, a royal priesthood, a dedicated nation, [God's] own purchased, special people, that you may set forth the wonderful deeds and display the virtues and perfections of Him Who called you out of darkness into His marvelous light (1 Peter 2:9 AMPC).

The enemy also wants bodies in which to live. Evil spirits want to connect with us, own us, and express their nature through us. The devil wants to express his evil nature in thoughts, words, and actions.

God's Goal: Connect → Own → Express

Consider the Gadarene demoniac. Jesus and His disciples crossed the Sea of Galilee and came to the region of Gadara. As soon as they got out of the boat, they encountered a demon-possessed man who appeared wildly insane. The enemy had made a connection, the demons took control, then expressed their personalities through the man.

The Enemy's Goal: Connect → Own → Express

> *And when He had come out of the boat, immediately there met Him out of the tombs a man with an unclean spirit, who had his dwelling among the tombs; and no one could bind him, not even with chains, because he had often been bound with shackles and chains. And the chains had been pulled apart by him, and the shackles broken in pieces; neither could anyone tame him. And always, night and day, he was in the mountains and in the tombs, crying out and cutting himself with stones* (Mark 5:2-5).

The enemy only has two doors to gain access to the believer—the emotion door and the thought door. He will try to get us to believe a lie or give into a negative emotion from the outside atmosphere. For example, there might be an emotional atmosphere of depression, irritation, or fear, but we can maintain inner peace even when an unpleasant environment surrounds us.

> *Be strong in the Lord, and in the power of His might* (Ephesians 6:10).

Make a distinction: That's not me. Start from the place of the new creation you, fused together with Christ (see 2 Corinthians 5:17). Make a distinction between the new creation you and the thoughts and impressions that the world, flesh, or the devil want to impose on you. The new creation loves God and loves His Word and always agrees with God. Anything that does not line up with the nature and character of God in you originates from either your flesh or demonic hitchhikers, not the real you!

If you hear a thought that doesn't sound like the new creation, don't accept it. It doesn't matter if a negative thought comes from your flesh or the devil. If it isn't something God would say, don't receive it. Say, "That's not me!"

Make a distinction: Inside or outside. Differentiate between flesh and demonic influence. It is vital to know the *source*—flesh or spirit. We can't cast out flesh and we can't sanctify a demon. When we have peace inside, we can resist anything negative on the outside. Yield or *submit* to Christ within, stay in peace, and *resist* external oppression. "I hear you knocking but you can't come in!"

- ***Check inside.*** When we feel oppression, or hear an intrusive thought, we should first check *inside*, in our gut. We feel our emotions *inside* us. We recognize demonic involvement by what we feel *outside* us. When we feel a negative emotion inside, we should always deal with our emotions first through forgiveness. Pray "first, feel, forgive." We can't resist unless we first have peace. Peace is the place of power.

- ***Check outside.*** When we have peace but perceive *outside* oppression, the pressure is external. As soon as we have peace, we are submitting (yielding) to God. Now we have the spiritual authority and strength to resist. We submit to God, resist the devil, and he has to flee. We already have victory when we are in the place of peace.

[S]ubmit to God. Resist the devil and he will flee from you (James 4:7).

As we become more proficient in exercising the five functions of our spirit, our spiritual strength increases. Things that once made us have a meltdown or greatly irritated us will eventually seem like slight annoyances that we can easily resist. Ever-increasing peace becomes a way of life.

Nothing can stop the flow of the river except a barrier in us. The river of God is an artesian spring—water under pressure. As long as we are open, the river flows. Only a barrier in us can block the flow. We get out of the way and the fountain gushes forth. *"[W]hoever drinks of the water that I shall give…will never thirst. But the water that I shall give him will become in him a fountain of water springing up into everlasting life"* (John 4:14).

Nothing can stop the flow of the river except a barrier in us.

CHAPTER 11

PLANTED BY THE RIVER

By Dennis

Every person is a "seed" sown from the heart of God into the earth. Within that seed is a spirit. We are not humans who have spiritual experiences; we are spirit beings having a human experience. Because we are the seeds of Heaven (see Matthew 13:37), we have access to the divine nature of God. Our citizenship is in Heaven. The Lord sows good seeds into the earth to partner with Him in advancing His Kingdom. At the end of the age, they will shine like stars with the brightness of His glory (see Daniel 12:3) *"The field is the world, the good seeds are the sons of the kingdom"* (Matthew 13:38).

> *"The good seeds are the sons of the kingdom."*

TREE OR TUMBLEWEED

Seeds must be planted to grow. Even if we make sure a seed has adequate sunshine, water, and fertilizer, it won't grow unless it's planted. We can speak to the seed, prophesy over it, pray for it, and confess the Word of God over it, but it will never grow until it's planted. It is impossible for the seed to grow if it is not planted. All the potential in that seed would remain just that—potential.

When a seed is planted under the right conditions with good soil, a water supply, and adequate sunlight, germination begins and the hard, outer shell cracks open. The first outward sign of growth is the formation of a root, which grows downward, anchoring the plant in the soil. Next, a stem with embryonic leaves pushes upward until it breaks through the surface of the soil. Then, and only then, a tiny oak tree begins to emerge.

The Scriptures teach many spiritual principles in types, allegories, and parables. Jesus often taught about the Kingdom of God using parables about seeds, soil, wind, plant growth, and harvest. Jeremiah 17:7-8 likens believers to trees and describes the conditions required for healthy growth:

> *But blessed is the man who trusts me, God, the woman who sticks with God. They're like trees replanted in Eden, putting down roots near the rivers—never a worry through the hottest of summers, never dropping a leaf, serene and calm through droughts, bearing fresh fruit every season* (Jeremiah 17:7-8 MSG).

When the Lord attends to our planting, we are likened to a tree planted by a river, whose roots go deep in the well-watered soil, and we won't be afraid when we face the trials of life. Why? Our roots give us stability and drink in life-giving water. Our heart is at peace regardless of circumstances, and we will produce abundant fruit in all seasons of life.

We are like trees replanted in Eden.

Notice that healthy trees are not self-planted. They are planted by God! Many choose the church they will attend based on convenience or personal preferences. Instead, we should ask the Lord to show us where He wants us to be planted. *"They will be called oaks of righteousness, a planting of the Lord for the display of his splendor"* (Isaiah 61:3b NIV).

The decision you make concerning where you are to be planted cannot be made on the basis of personal convenience. It must be based upon the principles that govern the kingdom of God…. I believe the Spirit of God desires to lead and guide us in the decision of the local church in which we are to be planted. God has a place that is just right for us and it will be exactly what we need in order to grow and mature in the Lord. He knows what type of ministry we need in order to be fruitful.[1]

Believers who thrive are planted in two ways. First, they are planted in Christ. They are *"firm, solid, and well-rooted, being by faith engrafted into Christ, and bringing forth fruit suitable to the soil wherein they are planted."*[2] Those who are firmly planted in Christ bring glory to God, and they themselves express His glory. They become witnesses who reveal God to the world.

Secondly, they are planted with God's people. The next requirement for healthy growth is having a healthy church home. *"Strangers* [Gentiles] *shall stand and feed your flocks, and the sons of the alien* [Gentile] *shall be your plowmen and vinedressers"* (Isaiah 61:5 KJV). The word *flock* refers to church homes that provide life-giving spiritual nourishment and do the work of spiritual husbandry, *"plowmen and vinedressers,"* for healthy growth. Healthy trees are planted with other trees.

Healthy trees are planted in Christ.

> *I will open rivers in desolate heights, and fountains in the midst of the valleys; I will make the wilderness a pool of water, and the dry land springs of water.* **I will plant in the wilderness the cedar and the acacia tree, the myrtle and the oil tree; I will set in the desert the cypress tree and the pine and the box tree together**, *that they may see and*

*know, and consider and understand **together**, that the hand
of the Lord has done this…* (Isaiah 41:18-20).

The Lord plants many trees of various kinds together to make
a sheltering forest. God brings us together with the people of His
choosing to build His church so we can
Healthy trees are planted   grow together. We were never intended
with other trees.   to live isolated lives. *"[L]et us consider
one another in order to stir up love and
good works, not forsaking the assembling of ourselves together, as is the
manner of some, but exhorting one another…"* (Hebrews 10:24-25).

After we are planted, we must maintain a right heart attitude.
In the company of others, our heart is tested and our attitudes ex-
posed. Will we serve with love without a personal agenda? Will we
allow ourselves to be loved to healthy spirituality? Our heart must
be "knit" to the pastor and our church family. Only then can we
truly belong.

When we trust in God, our lives are blessed. Our roots spread
out and make us strong and stable. Living waters quench our thirst
and cause us to thrive. Our spiritual health will give us stamina
in times of testing and our lives will be
When we trust in God,   fruitful. On the other hand, if we fail to
our lives are blessed.   obey His word, we rob ourselves of the
blessings that could be ours.

When we don't listen to God, we face consequences. It's not
that God punishes us; we cause our own trouble. God clearly says,
"If you do this, you will be blessed. If you do that, life will not go
well for you."

Those who fail to be planted seem to become drifters like tumbleweeds, never in the right place at the right time. They suffer

from spiritual blindness. They are unable to see God's provision for them even if it's right before their eyes, and they never seem to make much spiritual progress or bear fruit.

> *Cursed is the strong one who depends on mere humans, who thinks he can make it on muscle alone and sets God aside as dead weight. He's like a tumbleweed on the prairie, out of touch with the good earth. He lives rootless and aimless in a land where nothing grows* (Jeremiah 17:5-6 MSG).

A young woman attended our church for more than a year. A member of the congregation provided a place for her to live rent free while she got on her feet financially. Numerous others helped her in many different ways. However, she never made a heart connection nor listened to sound advice. She kept moving from one job to another, never making enough to live on her own. Finally, she moved to another state unchanged and unappreciative of the help she had received. Those who fail to be planted are *"like a tumbleweed on the prairie.... [They are] rootless and aimless in a land where nothing grows"* (Jeremiah 17:6 MSG). God told me, "Fruitfulness is proportional to planting."

Many otherwise gifted Christians with tremendous potential are just tumbleweeds. They have no root and, therefore, they have no fruit. No real growth or lasting change occurs and, as a result, their lives are barren. We must find out where God wants us planted and stay there until we are sure God has another place for us. It is always wrong to leave a church because of unresolved offenses. When the Lord moves us, it is for "graduation" rather than an escape.

Fruitfulness is proportional to planting.

COMMITMENT AND SERVICE

For us to be planted properly, it requires commitment and service on our part. When I was a young believer, the Lord directed me to a certain large church. In my heart, I became *planted* in that fellowship of believers and began to serve the pastor by doing whatever I could, even though the pastor was completely unaware.

When a building program was initiated, I volunteered to help and carried concrete blocks at the building site with the heart attitude of honoring God and my pastor. It was unimportant for anyone to know what I was doing. God sees what we do in secret and that's enough. Eventually this pastor became my spiritual father and mentor. Years later, he encouraged me to start my own church, but my commitment was so strong that it took much confirmation from God before I was willing to leave.

One interesting phenomenon that Jen noticed since we planted our church (of course, I was a pastor long before the two of us met) is that obvious spiritual growth occurs only in believers who are planted in a local church. I concur. When Christians fail to walk in victory and peace, continually struggling with repetitive cycles of trouble and spiritual warfare, they need to check their roots.

Many have passed through our doors with a "mall mentality," drifting through Christianity, going from conference to conference and church to church, taking a little here and a little there, but never getting connected. They drift like tumbleweeds and don't seem to ever change in a healthy way. We often encounter such believers after a timespan of many years, and the lack of positive change in their lives is shocking. They haven't changed for the better and still struggle in the same areas of their lives.

God plants for *growth*. *"Grow in the grace and knowledge"* of the Lord (2 Peter 3:18). The Lord already knows where each one of us will grow best. A vital ingredient seems to be *heart commitment* to a family of believers. Therefore, we should earnestly ask the Lord to reveal which family of believers He has chosen for us. It is thrilling to see people get healed, healthy, and knit into our spiritual family.

God wants us to be planted so we can become healthy, strong, and fruitful. The Lord places us in church families so we will have supportive relationships, grow to be spiritually healthy, have oversight for discipleship, and learn how to live in a loving community. *"God sets the solitary in families"* (Psalm 68:6). **God plants for growth.**

Spiritual growth involves becoming Christlike in character, discovering our spiritual identity, and developing our gifts and callings. Next, we must learn to be part of something bigger than ourselves (see Ephesians 2:21). Christianity is all about relationship. When we are truly planted in a fellowship of believers, we become part of a family where we learn to love and serve one another. *"[M]ay the Lord make you to increase and excel and overflow in love for one another and for all people* (1 Thessalonians 3:12 AMPC). We also discover our corporate identity. Finally, we become part of the family mission and corporate gifts and callings emerge.

We can never reach our full potential when we only care about ourselves. Success, even in Christian ministry, can be selfish—but destiny always includes others.

God plants for *provision*. Provision includes *all* our needs, not just finances. *"Seek first the kingdom of God and His righteousness, and all these things shall be added to you"* (Matthew 6:33). That includes proper relationships. The most important decision we will ever make, apart from becoming a Christian, is choosing a spouse. When the time is right, God will bring the person He has chosen for you from the other side of the world if necessary. If we concentrate on becoming the best Christians we can be, the Lord will take care of the rest. The lesson to be learned is this: We don't have to "help God out" when seeking a marriage partner. As we are obedient to Him, and that includes obeying the scriptural principles in the Bible, He really does provide for all our needs!

In my first pastorate, I once observed an amusing scenario. We had a regular mid-week service, and one night a group of teenage girls showed up. Not many teenage boys were there. The very next week, the girls didn't come, but a group of boys did. They looked around in disappointment and said, "We heard there were girls here. Where are the girls?" The irony of it all is that they missed the very thing they were looking for because they weren't putting God first.

A number of years ago, when our daughter, Allison, was in the Navy, she spent the first two years in Puerto Rico. When she transferred to Norfolk, Virginia, she began searching for a church home. We told her God already knew where she should go and suggested she ask the Lord for guidance. Within one week, she called to tell us she had been in an elevator and overheard some people talking about the church they attended. Allison felt the presence of God, so she asked them where the church was located. She was convinced that this was God's choice for her and started to attend. God often guides us by the people He places in our life. He connects us by *divine appointments*, *divine connections*, *divine order*, and *divine purpose*.

God plants for provision.

1. A *divine appointment* is an encounter with a key person who has been specifically and unmistakably inspired by God (see Genesis 24:4,48).

2. A *divine connection* is a God-ordained relationship (see Genesis 24:61-67). Relationships brought together by God

may include friendships, spiritual covering such as pastoral, boss at a job, or husband and wife.

3. *Divine order* positions us in the right place, at the right time, with the right people for God's purposes. *"God places the solitary in families"* (Psalm 68:6 AMPC).

4. *Divine purpose* establishes God's plan. We enter into what God is doing.

For we are His workmanship, created in Christ Jesus for good works, which God prepared beforehand that we should walk in them (Ephesians 2:10).

Shortly after this, Allison called to tell us that her paycheck was held up due to a glitch and she was very worried about it. When the church members learned about the situation, the congregation spontaneously took up an offering for her that covered all her financial needs until her pay was released. *"Those who are planted in the house of the Lord shall flourish in the courts of our God"* (Psalm 92:13).

Allison said she learned three important lessons from this experience: First, it is a really good idea to listen to God. He does have a specific church for each one of us. Next, she learned that church family is a reality not just a concept. And most importantly, she learned that she could really trust God to care for her.

God plants for *fruitfulness*. When we are planted and in fellowship with other believers, the Bible encourages us to make our church family a priority (see Galatians 6:10). When we do, we grow spiritually and our harvest of fruit increases (see 1 Peter 1:22). Community has a way of working selfishness out of us and increasing love and compassion in us.

But the fruit of the Spirit is love, joy, peace, longsuffering, kindness, goodness, faithfulness, gentleness, self-control. Against such there is no law (Galatians 5:22-23).

We should become a faithful part of the family mission to perform righteous works: *"And let us consider how we may spur one another on toward love and good deeds, not giving up meeting together, as some are in the habit of doing, but encouraging one another..."* (Hebrews 10:24-25 NIV). Becoming a productive member of a church includes becoming part of the vision of the house, or what we call the "family mission."

A number of years ago, the Lord rescued our son, Jason, after he backslid and made a major mess of his life. He had once been good with finances but had got into serious debt due to toxic relationships, and hit bottom quite dramatically. We promised Jason

God plants for fruitfulness.

a place to stay in our home and assured him that God would provide. He arrived with not much more than the shirt on his back. Jason spent the first few months becoming spiritually healthy by turning his heart back to God and dealing with his internal issues (which also greatly improved his physical health).

Not only did Jason come into personal health, but he quickly became knit with our pastoral team and congregation and shared our passion to release spiritual how to's to the Body of Christ at large (our family mission). Before long, we ordained him and turned an area of our ministry over to him (TEAM Embassy). His teaching and preaching gifts have flourished, and he operates in a gift of discernment and discerning of spirits as a "watchman on the wall."

Jason also created an online school that currently has more than 1,200 students enrolled from more than 35 nations around the world. The school has prospered and now provides a ministry income for him. The Lord then brought a lovely young woman to our church. They soon married and now have two children. Recently, the Lord visited Jason and brought him into personal revival that is releasing great spiritual refreshing to our entire congregation in a move of holiness.

NOTES

1. Robert Gay, *Planted: Finding Your Place in the Church Today* (Lake Mary, FL: Creation House, 2004), 12–13.

2. John Wesley, "John Wesley's Explanatory Notes," Isaiah 61 Commentary; http://www.christianity.com/bible/commentary.php?com=wes&b=23&c=61; accessed September 14, 2017.

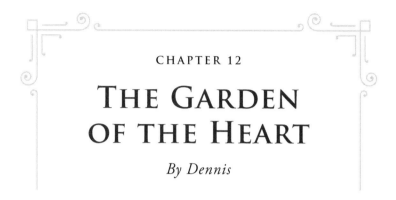

CHAPTER 12

THE GARDEN OF THE HEART

By Dennis

When we are born again, God claims our heart for Himself. However, much work is still necessary. Have you ever seen a garden that has gone to ruin? It is full of weeds and disorder. When we give our heart to God, He begins to deal with the weeds, set things in order, and advance His Kingdom of peace in our heart.

Not only must *we* be planted in a church home to grow, God desires to plant a fruitful garden *in our heart*. He sows His Word into the soil of the heart. To receive His Word, we must be in the place of peace. When we are at peace, our heart is open and receptive.

Scripture verses we know as mere information do not produce spiritual fruit in our lives. The Word of God bears fruit in us only by being *planted* in the soil of our heart. Even genuine revelation can be unfruitful. Revelation can be mental information, or it can produce heart transformation. Only revelation that takes root in our *heart* leads to spiritual growth.

Authentic Christianity is intimacy with God rather than sin management. It isn't about just being a good person or living a good life, but cultivating a deep dependency and trust in God.

The desire to depend on God goes against the ways of the world. When growing up, I wanted to become "independent" by the time I was nine years of age. I certainly didn't want Mom and Dad going into the store with me to buy things—I was a big boy and could do it all by myself. Independence, responsibility, and standing on our own two feet are considered maturity in the world's eyes, and they are good things.

The Word bears fruit when it is planted in our heart.

However, we mature in the Kingdom of God only by having intimate and direct fellowship with God. Through intimacy with Him, we become even *more* dependent upon the Lord, and we realize that apart from Him we can do nothing at all (see John 15:5). Developing dependence on God is healthy and necessary if we are to grow up and mature in Christ. In fact, becoming more and more dependent on God is what lays a foundation of trust. We step out in faith and trust God. He comes through for us, and we trust Him even more.

Fruitfulness brings glory to God.

We can be rich in Bible knowledge but still be unfruitful. It is good to know the Word but fruitfulness brings glory to God. We want Him to be able to inspect our tree and delight in an abundance of fruit.

WE ARE RESPONSIBLE

If we are not bearing fruit, it is no one else's fault but our own. We don't need more knowledge; we need truth that is planted more deeply. For those who say about the pastor's sermon, "I didn't get much out of the message," we must ask, "Did God tell you to be planted there?" If the answer is "yes," then He will give you what you need. If we get bored with what we're hearing, it usually means that the truth needs to penetrate our heart more fully.

God has a daily portion available for us, but it is our job to hear from Him and receive it. The phrase "daily bread" in the Lord's Prayer does not refer to food or material necessities, but to our spiritual sustenance—our daily portion of Him (see Matt. 6:11).

James admonishes us to *"receive with meekness the implanted word"* (James 1:21). The Word must be engrafted within us, meaning that direct spiritual contact has to be made on a heart level. God's Word only takes root as we have intimate contact with Him. We can't separate God's Word spoken to us from direct communion with Him. Careful hearing produces lasting fruit. Jesus preached everywhere He went, but it produced various yields in those who heard what was said. Everyone heard the same words, but some people responded with passion, some were indifferent, and still others became angry (see Matt. 12:14).

> *We don't need more knowledge; we need truth that is planted more deeply.*

Among even those who heard with gladness, there were different responses. Consider the 12 disciples. Peter, James, and John were the "inner circle," but John became the disciple *"whom Jesus loved"* (see John 20:2). It is a matter of the individual heart. Believers can too easily become sluggish or even hardhearted as believers. This is why Hosea encouraged Israel, *"Sow for yourselves righteousness; reap in mercy; break up your fallow ground, for it is time to seek the Lord, till He comes and rains righteousness on you"* (Hos. 10:12).

> *Careful hearing produces lasting fruit.*

If we don't allow our fallow ground to be plowed and made soft, all we have is dry crust. However, when we take God's Word to heart and cherish it like pure gold, then we will bear fruit. The seeds He plants will grow. The value we place on what we receive determines ultimate fruitfulness. If we consider something to be of little importance, it won't grow and develop. The vital factor is *how* we receive what was sown. Keep a record of those things spoken to you by the Lord. Write them down and make them part of your life.

PRACTICE

HOW TO RECEIVE A WORD

Close your eyes and pray. Focus on Christ in you (see Col. 1:27). Become quiet in the presence of God and wait for a while. Pay attention to the first verse of Scripture that comes to mind. Does the whole verse have "life" in it or does one particular phrase stand out? Don't do research or pick up a commentary.

Simply wait in the presence of God and welcome the "portion" He has for you. You want to meet the Author of that word, the Living Word. Allow God to plant it in your heart. It is a seed that God has planted. Write it down in your journal. Don't be a forgetful hearer, but stay open to that seed during the day. The next time you pray, start there. Don't hurry on to something else. Wait to see if the Lord amplifies it with other thoughts or verses and causes it to grow. Allow God to go to another subject when He wants, but let Him initiate.

A HEARING HEART

In addition to *receiving* a word, we must allow it to grow. Growth comes only as we *live* the word. Jesus tells a parable about a sower who went forth to sow seed, emphasizing the condition of the soil of the heart as a determining factor for fruitfulness.

Jesus told the Parable of the Sower to the crowds that gathered around to hear Him. In it, He emphasized the importance of our heart condition when it comes to fruit bearing. At the time Jesus told the story, it was a common sight to see a farmer sowing his field. He carried a sack filled with seed slung over his shoulder. He would reach into the sack and grasp handfuls of seed, tossing them in front of him as he walked.

> *Listen! Behold, a sower went out to sow. And it happened, as he sowed, that some seed fell by the wayside; and the birds of the air came and devoured it. Some fell on stony ground, where it did not have much earth; and immediately it sprang up because it had no depth of earth. But when the sun was up it was scorched, and because it had no root it withered away. And some seed fell among thorns; and the thorns grew up and choked it, and it yielded no crop. But other seed fell on good ground and yielded a crop that sprang up, increased and produced: some thirtyfold, some sixty, and some a hundred. And He said to them, "He who has ears to hear, let him hear!"* (Mark 4:3-9)

Some seed was sown by the wayside. In that day, well-worn footpaths ran beside farmers' fields with the soil compressed by foot traffic and passing carts. Some seed would inevitably land on the path where soil was so hard-packed that seed was unable to take root. Birds swiftly snatched away the seed that landed on such hard ground.

Other seed fell on stony places where the soil was shallow. The seed could put down a tap root, but it was impossible for deep roots to grow. A plant could sprout up, but as soon as the sun beat down upon it, it withered away. Without an adequate root system, plants quickly die from the heat and never produce fruit. Other seed landed on thorny weed-infested ground. Weeds and thorns are able to grow in even the rockiest and poorest soil. When seeds are sown among them, the thorns hinder growth and choke the life out of the tender sprouts of the good seed.

However, seed that lands on good ground does produce fruit, although in varying amounts. The amount of the yield can differ due to rainfall and temperature, but the seed can germinate and grow.

Sometime later, when the disciples were alone with Jesus, they asked Him about the meaning of the parable. He explained, *"To you it has been given to know the mystery of the kingdom of God..."* (Mark 4:11-12).

Jesus explained to His disciples that the parable refers to various conditions of people's hearts and their different responses upon hearing God's Word (Mark 4:14-20). When people's hearts are like hard soil, they can't understand and receive what they hear. It never takes root. Some people's hearts are like rocky soil—

The condition of the heart determines fruitfulness.

they hear and understand but they fall away when life gets tough. They forget what they heard. People with hearts like thorny soil receive what they hear, but the distractions and worries of life choke the life out so the tender sprouts can't grow and produce a harvest. Someone whose heart is like good soil hears and receives the word, which then takes root, grows, and produces fruit.

The Parable of the Sower teaches the importance of the condition of our heart. Our spiritual growth is impacted by the choices we make and the actions we take upon hearing the word of God.

HEARING REQUIRES OBEDIENCE

Many years ago, Jason, our son, had a dream and was given a prophetic word about a Bible school in the mountains that he should attend. It was clear he was hearing from God. When he finally got there, however, he began to have serious doubts. (Even if we receive a word from the Lord, it doesn't mean it will be easy to be obedient.)

The tuition was low because the students not only attended classes but did menial work. Rather than hire outside help, the school assigned the hard work of upkeep to the students. The men kept the grounds and did heavy labor. The women mopped, dusted, and did laundry. After a couple of weeks, Jason became quite indignant. He angrily called home to say God was telling him to leave the school.

Did God change His mind? No. However, it was so hard he thought he couldn't handle it. Fortunately, my son stuck it out, and it turned out to be an excellent experience for him. He was later elected president of his class based on Christian character. Attending the school was a vital step in making Jason the man he is today. However, that seed could easily have been stolen.

The person who receives a word and allows it to be planted will be given more. The law of increase takes effect. The way of obedience is the way to abundance.

> *The way of obedience is the way to abundance.*

INWORKING

How can we cooperate with God as He sows His word into our heart? We yield and absorb. That is the *inworking* of His word. We hear the word, allow it to become planted in our heart, and it becomes spiritual reality for us. The word we have received becomes something we believe and act on. It grows and produces fruit. How well we hear determines our fruitfulness.

CHOICES

First, we must make hearing a deliberate choice. It takes spiritual discipline and determination to make God our top priority. Scheduling a time for prayer is the *outward discipline* of setting aside time for God. We rarely find time for prayer if we don't plan for it. The *inward discipline* is prayer itself. We present ourselves to God and honor Him as a Person who is right there with us. In prayer, we spend time in the presence of the Lord. We listen to Him and enjoy being with Him. If we are too busy to spend time with God, how can we expect to hear from Him?

It takes spiritual discipline to make God our top priority.

Secondly, we need humility of heart. That alone will encourage us to spend time with God, because it forces us to realize how very much we need Him. David declared, *"As the deer pants for the water brooks, so pants my soul for You, O God"* (Ps. 42:1).

ABSORBING

Prayer is first of all being with a Person. It is *communion with God*. Begin with a time of silence so you can hear God. Yield your will to God. When you yield, you feel the "magnetic pull" of God in your heart drawing you closer to Him. If there are any blocks or issues you need to deal with, release them or receive forgiveness to get your peace back.

When you are in the presence of the Lord, first notice the nuances of His nature. It is important to pay attention to how the spiritual atmosphere feels around you. That is the portion of His divine nature He wishes to impart to you at that moment. Wait and pay attention. You may feel a gentle peace. However, you might sense joy, comfort, anticipation, fond affection, refreshing, or healing power.

What descriptive words surface to describe the atmosphere? Don't get back in your head at this point; just wait for whatever words come from your spirit. Briefly write them down in your journal but stay in prayer. Next, what Scriptures come to mind? Pictures? For

Prayer is being with a Person.

example, you may spontaneously see cleansing waters, an eagle soaring, a child being held by a loving parent, or a sunrise.

What is the Lord saying to you? What He speaks to your heart is your daily portion. Make a note of it, but hold it in your heart and let anointing "bathe" it. Continue waiting before the Lord and let Him "water" it with His presence. Write it down, remember it, make it part of your life, and share it with someone if the opportunity presents itself.

The next day in prayer, that is where you start—honoring the last thing God gave you. The seed has been planted and now you must allow it to grow. God will give the increase. *"Give us this day our daily bread"* (Matt. 6:11).

ATTITUDE

When we drink in, or absorb, what we have heard, we are birthing a new attitude. Attitude refers to the entire disposition of our heart, not a fleeting belief or behavior. This attitude is written on the tablet of our heart and becomes part of our character. God's thoughts, will, and emotions prevail. They take the ascendancy over our thoughts, will, and emotions. Isaiah reminds us:

"For My thoughts are not your thoughts, nor are your ways My ways," says the Lord. "For as the heavens are higher than the earth, so are My ways higher than your ways, and My thoughts than your thoughts" (Isaiah 55:8-9).

NATURE

Each time we receive a word planted by God in our heart, it begins to become part of who we are. It becomes part of our new creation identity. We have more of God's nature in our nature, and we are thereby growing *"in the grace and knowledge of the Lord"* (2 Pet. 3:18).

VALUE SYSTEM

Christ Himself living in us is our value system. We don't live by the law because He is the embodiment of Law. *"It is no longer I who live, but Christ lives in me"* (Gal. 2:20). Christ's life replaces

Christ's life replaces our life.

our life. Only Jesus can live the Christian life so we must live in complete dependence on Him. We then *"walk in the light as He is in the light"* all the while realizing that He can give us more light when we need it (1 John 1:7).

OUTWORKING

The key to the fruitful *outworking* of the seeds God has planted within the heart depends upon singleness of purpose in the pursuit of God. David declared his singleness of purpose in Psalm 27:4:

> *One thing I have desired of the Lord, that will I seek: that I may dwell in the house of the Lord all the days of my life, to behold the beauty of the Lord, and to inquire in His temple.*

We must allow God to demonstrate His life in us by the way we live. Our measure of fruitfulness will be determined by our hunger and diligence. A popular television talk show host once asked the audience, "Who wants to lose weight?" Almost every hand was eagerly raised. The host asked again, "Who is willing to do whatever it takes?" Most of the hands went down. Our question to you is, "Are you willing to do whatever it takes to pursue God and live a real Christianity?"

VALUE SYSTEM

The outworking begins with the final stage of inworking—the value system of God Himself within us. A strengthened foundation of trust allows God to express Himself through us. We cease trying to live the Christian life; the life of Christ flows through

our life. The river of His will can be released through us. We yield; God works.
We yield; God guides.

The life of Christ flows through our life.

*Lean on, trust in, and be confident in the Lord with all your
heart and mind and do not rely on your own insight or understanding. In all your ways know, recognize, and acknowledge Him, and He will direct and make straight and plain
your paths* (Proverbs 3:5-6 AMPC).

CHARACTER

We maintain a moment-by-moment trusting relationship with
God by staying in peace. When we lose our peace, it is instantly
restored through forgiveness. We must live a forgiveness lifestyle to
live in a continual flow of supernatural peace. Praying in the Spirit
during the day also helps us maintain a connec-
tion with God (see Jude 20-21). Our goal is to
let the peace of God *rule* in our lives (see Col.
3:15). When peace rules, Jesus rules.

When peace rules, Jesus rules.

*But if we walk in the light as He is in the light, we have fel-
lowship with one another, and the blood of Jesus Christ His
Son cleanses us from all sin. …If we confess our sins, He is
faithful and just to forgive us our sins and to cleanse us from
all unrighteousness* (1 John 1:7,9).

ATTITUDE OF GRATITUDE

Our *attitude*, in the sense we are using it here, is not merely
viewing something favorably or unfavorably. We also have a general mind-set that is a consistent predilection of our heart. For
example, the children of Israel had an angry and ungrateful attitude during their years in the wilderness. Whether we have a bad
attitude or a good attitude, we direct it first toward God. When

our heart is one with God's heart, we delight to do His will in all things. Gratitude always produces joy.

This joint labor of our will merged with God's will produces supernatural joy in our heart and a deep gratitude toward God. Paul reminds us, *"In everything give thanks; for this is the will of God in Christ Jesus for you"* (1 Thess. 5:18).

The will of God for your life is simply that you submit yourself to Him each day and say, "Father, Your will for today is mine. Your pleasure for today is mine. Your work for today is mine. I trust You to be God. You lead me today and I will follow."[1]

LOVE MOTIVATION

The love of God becomes our motivation. Righteousness is God's love in action. He moves our hearts, and our resulting deeds are acts of righteousness. When we listen and obey, the grace of God empowers us to do God's will. We desire to do His will out of love for Him and others rather than engaging in drudging religious duty. The *"love of Christ compels us"* (2 Cor. 5:14).

The love of God becomes our motivation.

BEHAVIOR

We must have the heart of Jesus see with the eyes of Jesus. We begin to see the gold in people rather than the dirt. When love motivates us, we have a redemptive mind-set to minister to and pray for others. In the process of helping people, however, it is important to guard against unsanctified mercy, which comes from our own ideas rather than the leading of the Lord. Jesus only did what He saw the Father doing.

God is the initiator of all actions that are truly righteous: *"For we are His workmanship, created in Christ Jesus for good works, which God prepared beforehand that we should walk in them"* (Ephesians 2:10).

EAT, DIGEST, AND ASSIMILATE

Many believers "church hop," moving from church to church, hoping to hear something new preached from the pulpits. We should come to let the Word of God get planted in our heart with the intention of applying it to our life. It should be our desire to take what we hear preached, pray about it, absorb it, and live it out to the best of our ability.

We should assemble at church to eat, digest, and assimilate the reality of Christ. Our church meetings are not for teaching as much as they are for feasting.

> *And Jesus said to them, "I am the bread of life. He who comes to Me shall never hunger, and he who believes in Me shall never thirst* (John 6:35).

We don't need deeper teaching; we need deeper heart change. God longs for us to be changed from the inside out. He desires to heal our hearts and bring us to maturity, not just to alter our outward behavior.

We don't need deeper teaching; we need deeper heart change.

TAKE HEED HOW YOU HEAR

When we carefully listen to God and receive His word, we reap in direct proportion to what is planted in our hearts. We will bear fruit according to what our hearts receive. When we read the Bible or pray, we should pay particular attention to whatever God quickens in our spirit, receive it, let it take root in us, and give it time to grow. When we cherish, absorb, and apply what we hear from God, we can anticipate an abundant harvest.

> *Therefore take heed how you hear. For whoever has, to him more will be given…* (Luke 8:18).

NOTE

1. Kay Arthur, Christian quotes on submitting your life to God; https://www
.christianquotes.info/quotes-by-author/kay-arthur-quotes/#axzz4tzjAXcwl;
accessed September 28, 2017.

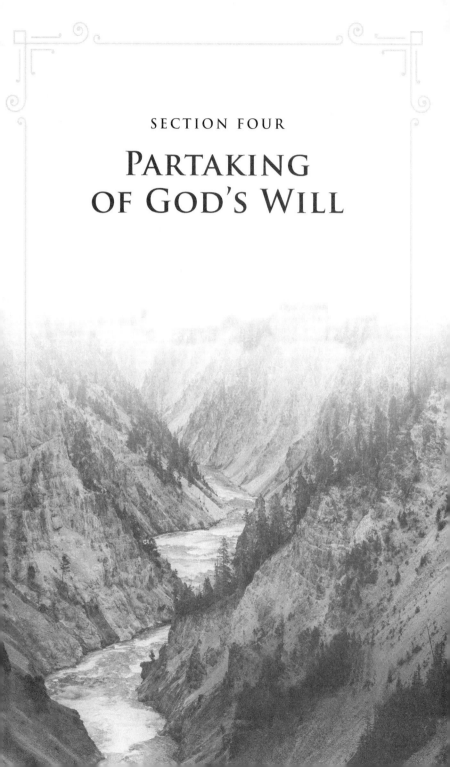

SECTION FOUR

PARTAKING
OF GOD'S WILL

CHAPTER 13

FEASTING ON GOD'S WILL

My food is to do the will of Him who sent Me, and to finish His work.—John 4:34

During the ministry of Jesus, the disciples had a temporal focus and were often concerned about their own physical needs. However, Jesus had entirely different priorities. Jesus encouraged them to *"seek first the kingdom of God and His righteousness"* and told them Father God would then supply everything they needed. His whole earth walk exemplified that very principle (see Matt. 6:33).

Following His conversation with Nicodemus about spiritual matters, Jesus departed from Jerusalem and traveled to the land of Judea where His disciples baptized those who came to Him in the Jordan River. From there, He and His disciples headed for Galilee, going directly through Samaria, and stopped on the outskirts of the city of Sychar. Jesus took a direct route north through Samaria rather than taking an indirect route that went around Samaria as did most Jews. Samaritans were no longer considered Jewish because of racial intermarriage and serious religious differences. It would be an understatement to say that they were greatly despised.

Moreover, they were almost as great in number as the Jews, which made the situation even more uncomfortable.

There was nothing haphazard about the route taken by Jesus that day. It was precisely planned to announce the dawn of a new day in the advance of the Kingdom of God (John 4:3-42).

Jesus entered the city and, wearied from His journey, sat down to rest at Jacob's Well. After His disciples departed to buy some food in town, a Samaritan woman came to the well to draw some water. Not only was she a Samaritan, but she was a woman, and a woman of questionable repute at that. Jews didn't speak with Samaritans, men weren't supposed to talk with a woman unless her husband was present, and rabbis certainly didn't have a conversation with a shady lady like this.

Breaking all the rules of propriety, Jesus struck up a friendly conversation with this woman and spoke profoundly into her life, promising a spring of life-giving water that gives eternal life and revealing details about her life that were known only to her. When the disciples returned with food to eat, they were shocked that He was conversing with a woman, and a Samaritan woman at that. As they stood there in amazement, the woman abruptly left her water pot by the well and rushed back into the city saying, *"Come, see a man who told me all the things that I ever did. Could this be the Christ?"* (John 4:29).

"Could this be the Christ?"

After the woman departed, the disciples said, *"Rabbi, eat."* Jesus said, *"I have food to eat of which you do not know"* (John 4:32). The disciples were perplexed at His statement. Surely He couldn't have already purchased some food somewhere and eaten it. Jesus further explained, *"My food is to do the will of Him who sent Me, and to finish His work"* (John 4:34).

"My food is to do the will of Him who sent Me, and to finish His work."

Knowing that they didn't understand, Jesus continued:

"Do you not say, 'There are still four months and then comes the harvest'? Behold, I say to you, lift up your eyes and look at the fields, for they are already white for harvest! And he who reaps receives wages, and gathers fruit for eternal life, that both he who sows and he who reaps may rejoice together. For in this the saying is true: 'One sows and another reaps.' I sent you to reap that for which you have not labored; others have labored, and you have entered into their labors" (John 4:35-38).

It seems likely that Jesus and His disciples were standing near a field of wheat when He spoke these words; wheat has white tips when ripe. However, Jesus wasn't referring to the wheat but to the multitudes that were making their way toward Him. As the disciples looked up, a crowd of people was coming toward them dressed in the typical white worker garments worn by Samaritans. A seed sown into the heart of one Samaritan woman had reaped a great harvest of souls.

Jesus was no longer hungry. Why? As Jesus did the work of His Father, the zeal of the Father in building His Kingdom became nourishing, supernatural food. He had feasted at the royal banqueting table! Jesus was able to continue ministering for two additional days in that town. Most individuals would have become exhausted, but Jesus was completely refreshed.

Simply doing more *work* didn't give Jesus more energy. He had spiritual food that sustained Him. This food was not only *knowing* the will of God, but actually *doing* it. Working the works of God was fully rejuvenating. What Jesus ate was supernatural nourishment that satisfied His physical needs and spiritually invigorated Him.

The story doesn't end here.

A study of this thrilling account would be incomplete if we did not notice the success of the Gospel among the Samaritans following the establishment of the Christian system. After the death of Stephen, the Jerusalem church was scattered abroad. In this connection, Philip the evangelist went to Samaria and proclaimed Christ (Acts 8:5). The multitude "gave heed with one accord" to his message, which was, incidentally buttressed with supernatural signs…. When the report of Philip's success came to the attention of the apostles up in Jerusalem, they sent Peter and John to Samaria, and the new converts were supplied with spiritual gifts to supplement their ministry (Acts 8:14). Subsequently, the Gospel was proclaimed in "many villages" of the Samaritans (Acts 8:25).[1]

The woman at the well became the catalyst for revival in Samaria that very day. What a marvelous thing! Jesus had accomplished His Father's work by bringing the Kingdom of God to these outcasts!

Of course, we receive spiritual nourishment from spiritual disciplines such as "eating" the Word of God, worship, prayer, and fellowship with believers. However, the greater food comes from co-laboring with God in Kingdom building. When His zeal becomes our passion, spiritual and physical strength energize us as we are about our Father's business. We are fed by what we *give* as well as what we receive.

We are fed by what we give as well as what we receive.

IF I COULD…

After pastoring for many years, it is common to look back and wonder what you could have done differently during that time. If you could do it all over again, what would you change?

If I (Dennis) had the opportunity for a do-over, I would teach believers to more fully understand the human will and the will of God. I believe the will is one of the least understood aspects of the Christian faith—and often *mis*understood. Many believers and leaders try to "do" the will of God. They attempt to live for God in their own strength, but it takes a great physical and emotional toll on them. They become tired, disillusioned, and discouraged. Many simply burn out after years of struggle and drop out of ministry.

The answer for this dilemma is revealed as we learn to practice the presence of God and allow Him to work through us. If we stop striving and enter the rest of God, peace can become our way of life. When we rest in God, we are in the river of His will.

The Scriptures promise us that there is help for our will. We are not on our own. Our responsibility is to cooperate by yielding to the Lord moment-by-moment. God says He will then *"cause,"* or empower, us to do what is right. We yield; He works.

> *Then I will sprinkle clean water on you, and you shall be clean; I will cleanse you from all your filthiness and from all your idols. I will give you a new heart and put a new spirit within you; I will take the heart of stone out of your flesh and give you a heart of flesh. **I will put My Spirit within you and cause you to walk in My statutes, and you will keep My judgments and do them** (Ezekiel 36:25-27).*

YIELDING TO GRACE

Most of us have been taught that grace is the unmerited favor of God. That is the most commonly used definition of grace.

Grace is Jesus living His life through us.

However, this definition fails to capture the full essence of grace. Grace is power. Grace is God's divine ability working in us. Grace is Jesus living His life through us. All we have to do is yield our will to Him.

> *And of His fullness we have all received, and grace for grace* (John 1:16).

The fact that John states that grace comes from His fullness teaches that grace is more than God's disposition or impersonal favor. It is God meeting us at our point of need in the Person of Jesus Christ, including all His power and provision.[2]

Grace empowers us to walk in the peace of God. We don't have to perform. It is God who gives us both the desire and the power to do His will. When we yield to God's grace within us, we get out of the way and let God be God. We are able to yield and do God's will.

THE POWER OF HEAVEN

Why would releasing the will of God through our life have a physical as well as a spiritual effect? The will of God contains the power and glory of Heaven—and that is what Jesus taught us to pray: that God's Kingdom would come on earth as it is in Heaven (see Matt. 6:10). Heaven is Heaven because the Presence of God is there and His will is done—nothing is obstructing it. When God works His will through us, we become portals through which Heaven is released.

The will of God contains the power and glory of Heaven.

God's will is the power of God at work. His *"kingdom and the power and the glory forever"* (Matt. 6:13). So, when we pray for Heaven to come to earth, we are asking that His presence would dwell among us and that His will and Kingdom would fill the earth.

INTERNALIZING THE WILL OF GOD

When we make a connection with Jesus in us, we touch His life. The Greek word for "life" in this passage of Scripture is *zoë*. It is also translated as "eternal life" and "everlasting life" because it refers to the life that comes from God. This is life as God in Himself has it, which is also in the Son. It is the present possession of the believer. However, we must yield to Christ in us to partake of heavenly life. "This life is not merely a principle of power and mobility, however, for it has moral associations which are inseparable from it, as of holiness and righteousness."[3]

God does not have "things" such as light, love, life, and power. God is light. God is love. God is life. He doesn't give us things; He gives us Himself through His Son. Christ is Light in us. He is Love in us. He is Life in us. He is Power in us. God made us to live by His life and do His works in the power of His life. Only those works that spring from zoë have value in the sight of God. Works done from any other source are "dead" works because they lack zoë. When we work the works of God, we plug into the power source of His divine life.

> *For we are His workmanship, created in Christ Jesus for good works, which God prepared beforehand that we should walk in them* (Ephesians 2:10).

Jesus said, *"My doctrine is not Mine, but His who sent Me. If anyone wills to do His will, he shall know concerning the doctrine, whether it is from God or whether I speak on My own authority"* (John 7:16-17). For God's will to become our food, we must desire to work the works of God. We must become active participants. God uses willing vessels. If we are willing to co-labor with God,

The question God asks us is, "Are you willing?"

He will teach us what He would have us do. We could teach an individual how to be born again, but the person must first be willing before something spiritual actually happens. We must yield and make God's will our will. The question God asks us is, "Are you willing?"

HUNGER AND THIRST FOR GOD'S WILL

Jesus offers us a satisfaction that comes only as a result of yielding our will to the will of Father God. Jesus promises: *"Blessed are those who hunger and thirst for righteousness, for they shall be filled"* (Matt. 5:6). Spiritual hunger is the deciding factor between those who see dramatic spiritual change in a few short months and those who see it over a period of many years.

We have seen individuals who passionately pursue their relationship with God and are radically transformed in a short period of time. Others change very little. Jesus rebuked the Laodicean church for their indifference. However, for those who were zealous and repented, He promised to dine with them: *"If anyone hears My voice and opens the door, I will come in to him and dine with him, and he with Me"* (Rev. 3:20). Those who hunger will be filled!

In the natural, when we are extremely hungry, we make finding food our main priority. It is the same way when we are hungry for God. Transformation in our Christian life is determined by our hunger and thirst for God.

Those who hunger will be filled!

When we become serious about the things of God, we get results. When we hunger and thirst after righteousness, we live a blessed life. There is a drastic difference between those who merely know information from their Bible and those who partake of God's spiritual feast.

THE LACK OF YIELDING

When we fail to yield to the grace of God within, we begin to work in our own power. When something unpleasant happens in the home, on the road, or in the workplace, too many believers put up a wall instead of surrendering to God's will.

Putting up a wall doesn't work. All it does is make us stressed out. That wall is a product of fear and control. We don't accomplish more. We simply wear ourselves out. Our own willpower is the source of our stress. Stress is epidemic worldwide, and the church is just as stressed as the world. One meaning of the word *trust* in Hebrew is *to run to someone for refuge*. We cannot be stressed and trust God at the same time.

We became particularly aware of the problem of stress in the church when we ministered in the New England states. It is true that native New Englanders inherited the blessing of a good work ethic from their Puritan forebears. However, a good work ethic must be sanctified through the lordship of Jesus Christ, or it can degenerate into frantic "busy-ness." We don't have to be "fried," or on the verge of burnout to have a good work ethic. The antidote for stress is found in the river of God's will.

Our willpower is the source of our stress.

The believers in the book of Acts worked most diligently to accomplish God's will yet didn't complain that they were burned out. They worked out of the rest of God (see Heb. 4:9).

SPIRITUAL FEAST

When we eat from the royal banqueting table prepared for us, it satisfies us.

We must not settle for information about God or religious traditions and rituals. True Christianity is fellowship with the Living God. Our level of satisfaction lets us know whether or not we are feasting on spiritual food. If we're wearied from trying to perform God's Word out of duty, we need a change of diet because God's will must be eaten and assimilated.

"He satisfies the longing soul, and fills the hungry soul with goodness."

The will of God *contains* His pleasure. As we feast on His will, His delight becomes our delight. We *"feast on the abundance"* of the King's house, and the Lord gives us drink from His *"river of delights"* (Ps. 36:8 NIV). If we become weary in our work, the Lord has a solution: *"He satisfies the longing soul, and fills the hungry soul with goodness"* (Ps. 107:9).

NOTES

1. Wayne Jackson, "Jesus and the Samaritan Woman," *ChristianCourier.com*; https://www.christiancourier.com/articles/282-jesus-and-the-samaritan-woman; accessed September 29, 2017.

2. Footnote for John 1:16: Spirit-Filled Life® Bible, Copyright © 1991 (Nashville, TN: Thomas Nelson Publishers), 1574.

3. W. E. Vine, *Vine's Expository Dictionary of Old and New Testament Words* (Old Tappan, NJ: Fleming H. Revell Company, Vol. 4, 1981), 336.

CHAPTER 14

PARTAKING OF HIDDEN MANNA

By Jen

Manna was a miracle food provided by God for the children of Israel during their years in the wilderness (see Exodus 16:14-16). It points to Jesus as the bread of life in the New Testament (see John 6:35). A small portion of this manna was offered back to God and placed in the Holy of Holies in a golden pot hidden inside the Ark of the Covenant (see Exodus 16:33; Hebrews 9:4). It was manna that was, in a sense, hidden. Gold represents the divine nature and manna signifies life-giving sustenance. The only person who had access to the manna in the Holy of Holies was the High Priest who entered only once a year. The term *hidden manna* is found only in the book of Revelation 2:17 in the letter to the church at Pergamos.

The purpose of the book of Revelation is to reveal the Lord Jesus Christ. The first chapter in the book of Revelation describes the proper ground of the church. The apostle John, who has been exiled to the island of Patmos, is in the Spirit on the Lord's Day. He heard a voice with a sound of *"many waters"* telling him to write all that he sees. Jesus reveals Himself to John as the Ancient of Days in His appearance, character, attributes, and His supremacy as Lord, divine Judge, and Redeemer. He calls Himself the Alpha and Omega, the Beginning and the End, who inhabits eternity.

The Lord stands in the midst of seven golden lamp stands, which is a picture of Christ in the midst of His church. In His hand are seven stars, and a two-edged sword comes out of His mouth. The seven stars are the angels, or messengers, of the seven churches. The Lord Jesus is the Light of the world and His assemblies are light bearers.

In the second and third chapters, the emphasis shifts to *eating spiritual food*. A promise is given to the Ephesian church that those who overcome will be permitted to eat from the tree of life (see Revelation 2:7). The third church, at Pergamos, is promised hidden manna. And Jesus tells the seventh church at Laodicea, *"I stand at the door and knock. If anyone hears My voice and opens the door, I will come in to him and dine with him, and he with Me"* (Revelation 3:20). However, all seven churches are cautioned to have an "ear to hear," which refers to the way we eat spiritual food. We must have peace before we can have an "ear to hear."

Church meetings should not be centered around teaching alone, but places to feast on Christ Himself. He is the tree of life and the hidden manna. When we assemble as a congregation of believers and feed upon Christ, we experience true satisfaction. We gather together to encounter the Lord and dine on heavenly nourishment.

Churches are places to feast.

HIDDEN MANNA AND A WHITE STONE

To understand the significance of the hidden manna, we must consider Jesus's letter to the church at Pergamos (see Revelation 2:12-17). It was the most spectacular Greek city in Asia Minor, located about 15 miles from the Aegean Sea, chief center of pagan religion, corrupt culture, and intellectual study, and, perhaps the greatest center of pagan worship at the time.

The temple of Zeus was there, as well as temples to many other pagan gods. The Christians there were surrounded by an evil culture. Pergamos was also the location of the Library of Pergamum, which contained more than 200,000 books containing much on ungodly philosophies. The church was rebuked for worldliness and idolatry. Instead of feasting on the Living Word, they were consuming *"doctrines of demons"* (1 Timothy 4:1; Hebrews 13:9; 2 Peter 2:1).

The Greek word *Pergamus* comes from *pergos*, meaning "elevated tower" and *gamos*, meaning "married." The church in Pergamos was rebuked for compromise with the world. Rather than building a dwelling place for God according to His blueprint (see Ephesians 2:22), they allowed the foundation to be corrupted. Instead of honoring their "marriage" with God, they were committing spiritual adultery with the world.

Jesus identifies Himself to them as the One with a two-edged sword. The sword comes out of the mouth of Jesus (see Revelation 1:16) and represents the words of Jesus (see Ephesians 6:17; Hebrews 4:12). In Hebrews 4:12-13, we learn that the Word of God is alive and full of power. The Word of God is not ink on a page, but a living Person, the Living Word: *"all things are naked and open to the eyes of Him to whom we must give account."* The sword has two functions. First, it severs the connection between the church and the world. Next, it judges the church joined to the world.

The church at Pergamos demonstrated loyalty to the *name* of Christ. The Greek word used here for "name," *onoma*, means all the name implies: excellence, sovereignty, divine nature, character, rank, power, and majesty. The church did not deny the true faith, which means they adhered to the Scriptures. They also stood fast in the time of persecution. It wasn't that they didn't know and love God. They just did not have the necessary zeal for the purity

The Word of God is alive and powerful.

of God's house, which was demonstrated by Jesus in the cleansing of the Temple (see Matthew 21:13).

Jesus rebuked the church for tolerating the doctrines of Balaam and the Nicolaitans. *Balaam* means "not of the people." The spirit of Balaam seeks to seduce the people of God and cause them to compromise with the world. Balaam was a false prophet from whose spirit came words that released death. On the other hand, the words of Jesus impart the life of God.

> Balaam was a prophet who was greedy for wealth. Today there are many people who come out to preach for the sake of money. Balaam's teaching was intended to cause the Israelites to unite with the Gentiles. Today there are also many people who advocate a union with the world. Balaam was hired by Balak, and in the same way, ever since Constantine joined Christianity, many have been "hired" by rulers. The consequences of Balaam's teaching were: (1) "to eat idol sacrifices," that is, to mingle with other religions; and (2) "to commit fornication," that is, to make friends with the world.[1]

This teaching separated the church from its true Head and exalted a false prophetic voice. According to second-century traditions, the Nicolaitans were false apostles who taught that Christ was a heavenly being, but Jesus on earth was a mere man. They also believed the apostolic teachings of Scripture were subordinate to new revelation from the Holy Spirit. The word *nicolaitans* in the Greek means "followers of Nicolas." *Nicolas* means "conquerors, or overcomers, of the people." Many Bible scholars believe the Nicolaitans were false apostles who taught false doctrine and propagated heresies.[2] False apostles rule with a heavy hand. True apostles equip believers and undergird them rather than rule over them. Because of this teaching, a hierarchical system was introduced in which religious leaders ruled over the members rather than equipping them to be fully functioning members of the Body of Christ.

Apostles are commissioned to take oversight as Christ builds His church. They are responsible to hear God's voice, build according to God's blueprint, and cooperate with the Holy Spirit in setting the living stones in place. The apostle Paul called himself a "wise master builder" who was responsible to lay the foundation of the churches he planted (see 1 Corinthians 3:10). The church is built upon *"the foundation of the apostles and prophets, Jesus Christ Himself being the chief cornerstone"* (Ephesians 2:20). It is impossible for Christ to build His church upon a foundation of false prophets and false apostles, but the church at Pergamos tolerated false teachers and allowed them to remain in the church.

> *But I have a few things against you, because you have there those who hold the doctrine of Balaam, who taught Balak to put a stumbling block before the children of Israel, to eat things sacrificed to idols, and to commit sexual immorality. Thus you also have those who hold the doctrine of the Nicolaitans, which thing I hate. Repent, or else I will come to you quickly and will fight against them with the sword of My mouth* (Revelation 2:14-16).

PROMISES TO OVERCOMERS

Jesus made three promises to those who repent and overcome.

> *He who has an ear, let him hear what the Spirit says to the churches. To him who overcomes I will give some of the hidden manna to eat. And I will give him a white stone, and on the stone a new name written which no one knows except him who receives it* (Revelation 2:17).

First, the overcomers are promised hidden manna. All believers can feast on the spiritual sustenance found in fellowship with the Lord. However, the hidden manna is reserved for those who commune with God in the Holy of Holies. *"To him who overcomes I will grant to sit with Me on My throne, as I also overcame and sat down with My Father on His throne"* (Revelation 3:21). They have eaten Christ, digested Him, and assimilated Him to the point that they are beyond the reach of the world, trying circumstances, and the enemy because of the great depth of their peace. They are *"hidden with Christ in God"* (Colossians 3:3). To these, God reveals His secrets because they live only to do His will. As such, they are co-laborers with God in the advancement of His Kingdom on earth.

The hidden manna is also a memorial, or reminder, of the bread God sent from Heaven. When we partake of Christ and have eaten, digested, and assimilated Him at the center of our being, we can become a place where God can dwell in His fullness (see Ephesians 3:17-19). As such, we are prepared to be built up into a *"holy temple in the Lord, in whom you also are being built together for a dwelling place of God in the Spirit"* (Ephesians 2:21-22).

Overcomers are promised hidden manna.

WHITE STONE

Secondly, those who overcome are promised a white stone. Just as manna was provided in the wilderness, 12 precious stones were fastened in the breastplate of the high priest, and upon each was inscribed the name of one of the 12 tribes. Although the meaning of the white stone is the subject of scholarly debate, one author proposes this meaning: "The white stone presumably is a sparkling diamond, perhaps answering to the *Urim* ('lights') also worn in Aaron's breastplate (Leviticus 8:8)."[3] The living stones of the New Jerusalem are not ordinary pieces of rock (see Isaiah 54:12-13; Revelation 21:19-20). God builds with precious jewels.

The high priest wore all these stones when he came into the Holy of Holies in the presence of God. Out of the tribe of Levi, God chose a loyal and dedicated remnant to minister to God in the Holy of Holies. *"But the priests, the Levites, the sons of Zadok, who kept charge of My sanctuary when the children of Israel went astray from Me, they shall come near Me to minister to Me"* (Ezekiel 44:15). Like the faithful Zadok priesthood, those who become intimate with the Lord come out of the world and are set apart wholly for God (see Ezekiel 44:15-31). God Himself is their inheritance.

Finally, the overcomers are promised a new name. God gives His hidden one a new name chosen by God Himself. It is a "name of special communication and fellowship known only to the Giver and receiver, a name reflecting…service for Him in this world and the world to come."[4]

God builds with precious jewels.

HIDDEN PORTION

We find different levels of eating in the wilderness that correspond to how close we come to the Lord. Everyone could eat the open manna but the diet changed for those who entered the Tabernacle of Moses. In the outer court, the Levites ate the meat of sacrificed animals. In the Holy Place, the priests who ministered there ate the showbread, or bread of the Presence. It was food only for the priests and could only be eaten in the Holy Place. Just one person, the high priest, could partake of the hidden manna in the Holy of Holies. He entered one time a year on the Day of Atonement and ministered directly to God with no separation. So we see that there are degrees of intimacy all related to eating.

The hidden portion of manna in the golden pot represents the rich experience of truly knowing the hidden Christ. This blessing is reserved for those who have forsaken the world to continually live in God's presence, partaking of His divine nature. The hidden manna is reserved for those who are so close to God that His desires are their only desires. When God Himself is our chief delight, our heart becomes so enraptured with Him that we want only what He wants (see Psalm 37:4). Our will becomes fully joined to God's will in a romance of wills.

> If we would understand what the hidden manna, the manna in the golden pot, is, we must understand a basic concept in the Bible, a concept which most Christians have not grasped.... According to Genesis 1 and 2, the basic requirement for living in the presence of God is to eat properly. What matters the most in God's presence is what and how we eat. Hence, in the Bible eating is a basic concept concerning our relationship with God. God has created everything, including man. If He can make the heavens and the earth and billions of items, what is there that He cannot do? He can easily do everything. Actually, there is even no need for Him to do anything, for He just speaks and what He desires comes into being. Nevertheless, there is one thing which God cannot do—He cannot eat for us. Although a mother may do many things for her children, she cannot eat for them. The children must eat for themselves. As far as our relationship with God is concerned, the basic matter is eating properly.[5]

Jesus said He had spiritual food that sustained His life. This same food is offered to those who live in wholehearted commitment to God. They are the answer to the prayer for Heaven to be released on earth, because they themselves have become portals through which the glory of God pours forth (see Matthew 6:10).

For I have come down from heaven, not to do My own will,
but the will of Him who sent Me (John 6:38).

The will of God contains His pleasure, so the doers of His will have the joy of Heaven effervescing within them (see Ephesians 1:5-9; Philippians 2:13). Hidden manna is food for those who love and do God's will.

They boldly approach the throne of grace in the Holy of Holies to know and be known by God (see Hebrews 4:6). The epitome of God's will is not working for Him but communion with Him. Jesus commended Mary of Bethany because she sat at His feet in humble adoration (see Luke 10:39-42). Her reward was Christ Himself. Jesus praised Mary, saying, *"Mary has chosen that good part, which will not be taken away from her."*

> *Hidden manna is food for those who love and do God's will.*

God reveals Himself to those who draw near and partake of Him. *"Blessed are those who hunger and thirst for righteousness, for they shall be filled"* (Matthew 5:6).

NOTES

1. Watchman Nee, *Collected Works of Watchman Nee, Vol. 16: Study on Revelation* Chapter 3, (Anaheim, CA: Living Stream Ministry, 1992; Watchman Nee, "The Church in Pergamos," Living Stream Ministry; https://www.ministrybooks.org/books.cfm?xid=ESRND29IF1XAU accessed August 4, 2017.

2. H. M. Morris, *The Revelation Record* (Wheaton, IL: Tyndale House Publishers, 1986), 51–52, 58; "The 'Nicolaitans' are mentioned only here and in Revelation 2:15. There was no known sect or movement with this name during the apostolic period, so this is probably a descriptive term rather than a proper noun. Since these messages were meant ultimately for all churches, it is certain that the term has meaning for all churches. In context, it almost certainly is referring to the false apostles of Revelation 2:2. Practically all churches have been plagued at one time or another by false teachers, false prophets, false apostles, and sometimes even by false christs. The term 'Nicolaitans' means literally 'overcomers of the people.' That, of course, is precisely what false

apostles seek to do, desiring to turn the love and allegiance of the people in the church to themselves rather than to Christ. Christ hates both the deeds and doctrines (Revelation 2:15) of Nicolaitanism, and we should do the same." Institute for Creation Research, "Nicolaitans" (June 4, 2014); http://www.icr .org/books/defenders/8969/; accessed September 28, 2015.

3. H. M. Morris, *The Revelation Record*, 59.

4. Ibid.

5. Witness Lee, *Life-Study of Hebrews*, (Anaheim, CA: Living Stream Ministry, 2011, first published 1984), 643.

THE PINNACLE OF GOD'S WILL

CHAPTER 15

VESSELS OF GOD'S WILL

*I will give you a new heart and put a **new Spirit** within you….*—Ezekiel 36:26

In seeking the will of God, Jesus is our example. He lived on earth in complete dependence on His Father and did nothing apart from Him. His obedience was perfect. The Spirit of Holiness rested upon Him and remained. Father God pronounced His approval at both the beginning and end of the Jesus's ministry by saying, *"This is My beloved Son, in whom I am well pleased"* (see Matthew 3:17; 17:5).

When Jesus lived on earth, He was the perfect expression of His Father. *"He who has seen Me has seen the Father"* (John 14:9). We were created by God to be expressions of the Father—just like Jesus.

God loves us unconditionally; even when we fail to appropriate all He has for us, He loves us. However, He rejoices when we choose His best. God's best is the ultimate intention He purposed in His heart for humankind—His eternal purpose. He created us to live by the life that is in Christ, be conformed to His image, and enter into the glory of Christ as coheirs with Him as a real experience, not just doctrine (see Romans 8:17, 29).

> From eternity past up to the resurrection, the Lord is the only begotten Son. But after He is raised from the dead He becomes the firstborn Son. Accordingly, after the resurrection He says this to Mary Magdalene: "Go unto my brethren, and say to them, I ascend unto my Father and your Father" (John 20:17). By the death of God's only begotten Son, many sons are born.... God takes His Son as the mold or stamp, and in this stamp God impresses us many sons so that His Son might be the firstborn among many sons. He causes us to have the glory of His Son as well as the life [and nature] of His Son (Rom. 8:29-30).[1]

We were created by God to be expressions of the Father—just like Jesus.

CREATED AS CONTAINERS

We were created in God's image to be vessels, or containers, of God's Spirit to walk as Jesus walked. Unlike animals, which only have biological life, we must have a spirit in us to live. *"The body without the spirit is dead"* (James 2:26).

We are a derivative life requiring a spirit to dwell in us. We merely express the spirit, filling us. A vessel is designed to be *filled* with something. Otherwise it serves no purpose. In our case, we are designed to contain *Someone* (see Ephesians 3:19). The Scriptures call us vessels, branches of the vine, and temples of the Holy Spirit.

We were formed to be containers of an indwelling spirit.

These symbols used to describe us humans are all those which express no nature of their own but as means of expressing that to which they are attached. Vessels contain the liquid, but are not the liquid; the cup is not the coffee. We don't speak of a cup and coffee. So we are branches; but the branch is not the nature but the vine which reproduces itself in leaf and fruit form on the branch.[2]

Spirit can mix with spirit, or *interpenetrate*, unlike physical matter. When a carpenter makes a chair, he does not become part of the chair. It is impossible. However, it *is* possible for us to be in union with God. We are spirit beings made *"in the image of God"* (Genesis 1:26-27). In receiving the Spirit of Christ, we are *"joined to the Lord"* and become *"one spirit with Him"* (1 Corinthians 6:17). Our spirit becomes one with His Spirit. "Our 'bodies are the temple of the Spirit, and God is spoken of as 'dwelling in us and walking in us'" (2 Corinthians 6:16).[3]

A REPLACED LIFE

Prior to the Fall, Adam and Eve were faced with a choice. Would they eat of the Tree of Life and be filled with the Holy Spirit, or eat from the Tree of the Knowledge of Good and Evil? They ate from the wrong tree. The devil stole God's property and filled them with a sin spirit—the spirit of error. All people inherited a wrong nature and became *"sons of disobedience"* and *"children of wrath"* due to Adam's disobedience (Ephesians 2:1-3).

From eternity past, God had a plan to reclaim what was His. In the fullness of time, God sent His Son to die for us that we might become sons and daughters restored to our Father! *"For God so loved the world that He gave His only begotten Son, that whoever believes in Him should not perish but have everlasting life"* (John 3:16). And: *"God demonstrates His own love toward us, in that while we were still sinners, Christ died for us"* (Romans 5:8).

How could fallen sinners be reconciled with a God who loves with holy love? God is love but He is also holy. He is *"of purer eyes than to behold evil"* (Habakkuk 1:13).

God is love. Love is the nature of God, not just something He has. From the very beginning, God loved with a perfect, unselfish love that exists to give. It is total self-giving love. With the Fall, human beings turned in on self and became self-loving selves. The nature of humanity apart from God is selfish and self-serving to the core. Love reached out to us fallen sinners and made a way to restore us to fellowship. Love seeks communion.

God is holy. Only God is holy. Holiness is not just one of God's divine attributes; it is the innermost essence of God. He doesn't have holiness as a "thing"—He is holy because it is His nature. In rescuing fallen humanity, God had to ***Love seeks*** satisfy the tension between love and holiness. Ho-***communion.*** liness separates God from everything unholy. Love seeks communion, but holiness requires separation. Holiness is both separation from all sin and separation unto God. Holiness is separateness, glory, and blazing purity.

When the prophet Isaiah encountered God in His holiness, the seraphs covered their faces and sang, *"Holy, holy, holy is the Lord Almighty; the whole earth is filled with His glory"* and Isaiah cried out, *"Woe is me, for I am undone! Because I am a man of unclean lips, and I dwell in the midst of a people of unclean lips; for my eyes have seen the King, the Lord of hosts"* (Isaiah 6:3, 5). The prophet was dumbstruck by the contrast between his sinfulness and God's holiness.

How can a holy God meet unholy us? God's plan of redemption provides the solution. He made provision for communion with His created ones through the work of Jesus on the cross. He satisfied His requirement for holiness through replacing our life with Christ's life.

Holiness requires separation.

TWOFOLD REDEMPTION

In Adam, we inherited two problems: *sins* committed and a *wrong spirit* filling us. In Christ, God provides a twofold redemption: the blood and the cross. We receive forgiveness of our sins through His shed blood. *"In Him we have redemption through His blood, the forgiveness of sins"* (Ephesians 1:7). Our second dilemma is the presence of a *wrong spirit* in us, or a sin nature, governed by the law of sin and death (see Romans 8:2). Therefore, we need a *new Spirit!* That is also accomplished by the work of the cross.

Jesus took all humanity with Him when He died on the cross. We died when He died. Because our spirit leaves our body when we die, the sin spirit, or nature, left when we died with Christ. *"The body without the spirit is dead"* (James 2:26). Because we died, we died to the infilling of the wrong spirit so we could be filled with another Spirit—the Spirit of God. When Christ was raised from the dead, we were raised together with Him with a *new spirit.* We received *"newness of life"* (Romans 6:4).

The indwelling sin spirit was *replaced* by the Spirit of Christ! When Christ was raised by the power of the Father, we were raised together with Him with a *new spirit.* Our life replaced by Christ's Life gives us:

The spirit of sin is replaced by the Spirit of Christ!

- The Spirit of Life instead of a spirit of death
- The Spirit of Truth instead of a spirit of error
- The True Vine (source of living) instead of a false vine
- The Spirit of Holiness instead of a spirit of sin

God doesn't make *us* good, because there is no goodness in us. God doesn't make *us* loving, because human love falls short of God's love. God doesn't make *us* holy, because only He is holy. For every need, God gives us Christ. *"[B]y His doing you are in Christ Jesus, who became to us wisdom from God, and righteousness and sanctification* [holiness], *and redemption"* (1 Corinthians 1:30 NASB). And: *"it is no longer I who live, but Christ lives in me"* (Galatians 2:20).

It was impossible for us to live the Christian life all along. "We are forced to admit that we cannot manifest godliness apart from God, or righteousness apart from the Righteous One, Jesus Christ. The Christian life is Christ's life lived out in us, as us, and through us, while we as dependent creatures derive [everything] from Him."[4] Through a Replaced Life, we no longer manifest a wrong spirit, but Christ's Spirit.

For every need, God gives us Christ.

> When Paul says we are raised with Christ, he is not speaking only of the resurrection. The resurrection was the beginning of Jesus's ascension, but Paul has more in mind than just the resurrection…. Paul clearly has the result of the resurrection and the ascension of Jesus in mind because he is thinking of Jesus's exaltation to heavenly places. This is the result of both His resurrection and His ascension.

> What is even more shocking than Jesus's own ascension is that Paul tells us that we have been raised up with Him. In other words, when Jesus ascended, we ascended. Paul describes this reality by using the past tense. We *have* ascended. It has already been accomplished. Paul is describing a governmental reality, not a metaphysical one.

He is not simply saying that we are raised up in our spirit. He is telling us that Jesus, as a man, has taken a governmental position and in doing so recovered the governmental position of man for all those who are in Jesus. We will be raised from the dead in the future, but we have already been raised positionally with Jesus. What man lost and forfeited in the garden in terms of his position and authority before God has been reclaimed.[5]

When we were born again, most of us received forgiveness of sins alone because that's all we understood. Christ becomes an influence in our lives, but we continue to struggle with sin by willpower as we *try* to live the Christian life (see Romans 6 and 7). Later, a second recognition comes. We not only need forgiveness but a *new* nature, or spirit!

> *I will give you a new heart and put a **new spirit** within you...* (Ezekiel 36:26).

Because we are vessels, or containers, not independent "selves," we cannot have two natures, or two spirits filling us. Only one spirit can fill our vessel. We can't be filled with the Spirit of truth *and* the spirit of error at the same time (1 John 3:24; 4:6). Our "self" is expressed by the spirit filling us. It is not possible to "die to self" in the sense that our self actually *dies*. We will always be a self. We simply die to one spirit only to be instantly filled with another Spirit.

Only one spirit can fill our vessel.

A STARTLING VISION

Almost 30 years ago, I (Jen) had a startling vision. I was a new believer who wanted to be transformed into a "child from another world" with all my heart. And yet, it was horrifying to me to discover that sin was still a struggle after salvation. How could I possibly be like Jesus? It seemed like the more I tried, the more I failed. Even when my outward behavior seemed commendable, my attitudes were often wrong.

My signpost individuals, even during my unsaved years, were those saints who seemed ever unruffled by the circumstances of life and seemed to dwell in a heavenly realm inaccessible to ordinary people. Even in novels like *Jane Eyre*, Jane did not interest me so much as the orphan girl, Helen Burns, who lived and died in the love of Christ.

One day, as a new believer, I found myself standing in the altar area after the church service. Suddenly Jesus appeared and we stood face-to-Face. As I gasped audibly, Jesus stepped toward me, put His hands on mine, and then, much to my amazement, He turned and stepped into me. His eyes were now my eyes and His heart my heart. I was overwhelmed with love at first, but the impression gradually faded away. Life went back to Christianity as usual. Three decades afterward, my experience still fell far short of that vision.

In summer of 2016, I finally understood the secret. It's not that I hadn't searched the Scriptures and pored over the many books written by saints of old. The Lord Himself must remove the veil that blinds our eyes, according to His timing. Discovering that I had been born a slave who needed a new Master was perhaps the most liberating revelation of my life next to the new birth. "*[H]aving been set free from sin, and having become slaves of God, you have your fruit to holiness*" (Romans 6:22).

The Lord began to reveal the mystery of my life replaced by Christ's life. His Spirit hovered over me for months and the word I wrote again and again in my journal was "overshadowed." I felt as though the Spirit of Holiness was hovering over me as in Genesis, and that He was preparing to birth something, or Someone, new in me (see Genesis 1:2; Luke 1:35; 9:34).

The following year a revival of holiness broke out in our church. And then just as in the vision, He came to live His life in me. The experience was mine.

We are born slaves who need a new Master.

THE TWO-NATURE FALLACY

Before we discover the mystery of Christ in us, we feel as though we have a bad dog and good dog constantly fighting within us. Many believers have believed this two-nature fallacy because this seemed true based on their experience. However, if that is true, what do we do with the following Scriptures from Romans 6?

> *"How shall we who died to sin live any longer in it?"* (v. 2).

> *"Our old man was crucified with Him, that the body of sin might be done away with, that we should no longer be slaves of sin"* (v. 6).

> *"He who has died has been freed from sin"* (v. 7).

> *"Sin shall not have dominion over you, for you are not under law but under grace"* (v. 14).

> *"Having been set free from sin, you became slaves of righteousness"* (v. 18).

> *"But now having been set free from sin, and having become slaves of God, you have your fruit to holiness"* (v. 22).

What about Romans 7? Is that the way we are doomed to live our Christian lives? Doesn't it contradict the freedom promised in Romans chapter 6? If so, why does Paul joyfully cry out in the final verse: *"I thank God—through Jesus Christ our Lord!* (Romans 7:25)? That hardly seems like the wretched man of verse 24 who still needed deliverance: *"O wretched man that I am! Who will deliver me from this body of death?"* Notice that Paul's question asked, *"Who?"* The very next part of the verse tells us that the way of deliverance is the Deliverer: *"Jesus Christ our Lord!"* We are rescued by the Person who takes our place!

Then what is Romans 7 really about? It's all about the "I" of self-effort. In Romans 6, we learn we've been delivered. In Romans 7, we see the futility of trying to live the Christian life through self-effort. We have been delivered from *trying* to keep the law by a Person who lives in us as the embodiment of the Law. *"It is God who works in you both to **will** and to **do** for His good pleasure"* (Philippians 2:13). If it's Christ in us willing and working, what is left for us to do? Thank Him and yield to Him!

We are rescued by the Person who takes our place!

We must point out that serious divisions have occurred in our churches over some of these subjects. Do we have it all at the new birth? Is there a second work? Is there one baptism of the Spirit or are there many? Does sin get permanently destroyed in us? Do believers have two natures fighting within them until they get to Heaven? How many works of grace are there? Should we baptize by sprinkling or immersion?

There are thousands, whole groups and denominations, whose beliefs on such points as these are diametrically opposed. Should that not be a warning to us not to be too fierce in our denunciations of others, nor too separate from them? Do we not get nearer the truth when we recognize that in all of us our hearts have gone farther than our heads? We can experience what we can only stumblingly expound. Once again we come back to what? A Person—the Lord Jesus Christ. Around Him we unite in our hearts' love, when our heads would keep us far apart.... Not with those who hold the same doctrines about Him, but those who love Him. There we unite.... [I]f there are so many convinced bodies of believers who hold passionately to their special viewpoints, it is because they each have something from God the whole body needs.... [A]ll opposites meet in Him, and all opposites have truth.[6]

Do we get all the riches of Christ at our conversion? Yes! Do we grow in our Christian faith progressively? Yes! Are there some things we will only understand in Heaven? Yes! Does God want us to love our brothers and sisters in Christ even if we disagree? Yes!

Could it be that in the next Great Awakening some or all of this will become clear by increased revelation from our Lord? He will further enlighten His body to remove some walls of division and inspire us to spiritual heights we have not yet experienced in fullness of Him and the blessing of unity in Christ according to the prayer prayed by our Lord Jesus in John 17.

> *[T]hat they all may be one, as You, Father, are in Me, and I in You; that they also may be one in Us, that the world may believe that You sent Me. ...I in them, and You in Me; that they may be made perfect in one...* (John 17:21,23).

In light of this, our position emulates that of the Moravians in Germany during the eighteenth century who were known for their love and unity.[7] These believers who actually experienced the answer to the prayer of Jesus for unity took as their motto: "In essentials, unity; in nonessentials, liberty; in all things, love."

Under Mosaic law, only the high priest could enter the Holy of Holies in the temple on one day of the year. However, the day of

Pentecost ushered in a new era. The early church displayed God's rule and reign in and through individuals. Now God was not confined to living in the midst of His people, He made people His temples (see 1 Corinthians 6:19)!

In all things, love. The three levels of the cross correspond to the three rooms of the Tabernacle of Moses and the Temple: outer court, Holy Place, and the Holy of Holies. The first room symbolizes living by human understanding, or the light of the sun. In the second room, we discover the light of revelation. Only in the third room does God Himself become our light: *"…They need no lamp nor light of the sun, for the Lord God gives them light. And they shall reign forever and ever"* (Revelation 22:5).

God's dwelling place multiplied from a physical location to the hearts of a multitude of believers. *"Your body is the temple of the Holy Spirit who is in you"* (1 Corinthians 6:19). Jesus no longer preached just in Israel, but His testimony would be preached and demonstrated through *believers* around the world through the power of the Holy Spirit.

CHILDREN, YOUNG MEN, FATHERS

In his first epistle, John the beloved likens the three great levels of Christian experience to *little children, young men,* and *fathers* (1 John 2:13-14). We inherit the fullness of all three levels at the time of initial salvation, but usually require further revelation to understand how to experience *"the riches of the glory of this mystery…which is Christ in you, the hope of glory"* (Colossians 1:27).

What do these levels signify? Little children are those who are saved because they have received forgiveness for their sins. A child lives in dependence on his parents and knows them outwardly. Little children live in self-effort knowing God is for them externally rather than living by Christ's life within. The second level is that of the young men who have *"overcome the wicked one,"* and Christ abides in them as the Living Word.

The third level, fathers, is those who know *"Him who is from the beginning"*—the Eternal One who now, as from the beginning, is com-

God made people His temple.

pleting His eternal purpose. Fathers are consumed by the eternal purpose of God in loving and redeeming others. Fathers volunteer to live sacrificial lives just as Paul did: *"If I am being poured out as a **drink offering** on the sacrifice and service of your faith, I am glad and rejoice with you all"* (Philippians 2:17). The third level is summit living—the level of the overcomers who have seen the door still open in Heaven and share the Throne (see Revelation 4:1; Revelation 3:21).

The entrance to each level is through the work of the cross and involves a counting of the cost. To those who would be His disciples, Jesus says, *"If anyone desires to come after Me, let him deny himself, and take up his cross, and follow Me. For whoever desires to save his life will lose it, but whoever loses his life for My sake will find it"* (Matthew 16:24-25).

FIRST LEVEL Forgiven Life	SECOND LEVEL Replaced Life	THIRD LEVEL Enthroned Life
"Little Children"	"Young Men"	"Fathers"
*In Him we have redemption through His blood, the **forgiveness of sins*** (Ephesians 1:7)	*I have been crucified with Christ; **it is no longer I who live, but Christ lives in me*** (Galatians 2:20)	*I beseech you therefore...that you **present your bodies a living sacrifice**, holy, acceptable to God, which is your reasonable service* (Romans 12:1)

WHAT ABOUT TEMPTATION AND SIN?

After coming into the experience of the replaced life, does sin go away forever? No. It simply loses its power over us. We must still deal with the duality of our humanity: Christ within but the world, the flesh, and the devil without. When we know that temptation is not sin, we don't feel condemned when we are tempted! Temptation is merely an opportunity for Christ to reveal His power working in us. *"My brethren, count it all joy when you fall into various trials* [temptations]" (James 1:2).

Temptation is inevitable. We live in a sinful world filled with sinful people and every kind of sinful enticement imaginable, so temptation is an inevitable part of human living: *"Each one is tempted when he is drawn away by his own desires and enticed"* (James 1:14). We are tempted when our mind and body are stirred up by our flesh. We are delivered from indwelling sin, but we are not out of calling distance.

We are kept by the power of God. Because we are now set free from the suspicion that temptation is sin *and* our response to it are both sin, we can relax in confidence that the power of God is strong enough to hold us close to Him. Temptation and sin *pull* on our flesh. However, the power of God has a **more powerful magnetic pull**. We are kept by *"the power of God"* indwelling us (1 Peter 1:5)! Jesus, the Son of God, was *"in all points tempted as we are, yet without sin"* (Hebrews 4:15). The truth you need to see

We are kept by the power of God.

is that anything Jesus did in His earth walk He can do through YOU! Therefore, when tempted, yield to Christ within and resist. *"Therefore submit to God. Resist the devil and he will flee from you"* (James 4:7).

Receive and Believe

We will be a "self" for all eternity. We just change from one master, *satan*, to another Master—the Lord Jesus Christ, expressing His life in us. In Christ, we *replace* a wrong spirit, *sin and death*, with the right Spirit: the *"Spirit of life in Christ Jesus"* (Romans 8:2). "There is a great difference between realizing, 'On that cross He was crucified *for me*,' and 'On that cross I am crucified *with Him*.' The one aspect brings us deliverance from sin's *condemnation*, the other brings us deliverance from sin's *power*."[8]

> What is the normal Christian life? The Apostle Paul gives us his own definition of the Christian life in Galatians 2:20. It is *"no longer I, but Christ."* Here he is not stating something special or peculiar—a high level of Christianity. He is…presenting God's normal for a Christian, which can be summarized in the words: I live no longer, but Christ lives His life in me. God makes it quite clear in His Word that He has only one answer to every human need—His Son, Jesus Christ. In all His dealings with us He works by taking us out of the way and substituting Christ in our place. The Son of God died instead of us for our forgiveness: He lives instead of us for our deliverance.[9]

As this truth is quickened to us, we simply receive and believe. Faith reaches out and grasps truth, thus bringing it into our present reality. *"I have been crucified with Christ; it is no longer I who live, but Christ lives in me; and the life which I now live in the flesh I live by faith in the Son of God, who loved me and gave Himself for me"* (Galatians 2:20). How do we receive the promises

Through faith and patience we inherit the promises!

of God? We believe until the object of our faith becomes reality. Through *"faith and patience"* we *"inherit the promises"* (Hebrews 6:12).

- Be steadfast in believing and confessing it as truth (see Romans 10:10).

- Hold on by faith until you receive the full reality (see Hebrews 10:23; 11:1).

- God will make it a real experience through a spiritual encounter.

NOTES

1. Watchman Nee, *God's Plan and the Overcomers* (New York, NY: Christian Fellowship Publishers, 1977), 12–13.

2. Norman Grubb, *It's as Simple as This* (Blowing Rock, NC: Zerubbabel Press, 2005), 8–9.

3. Ibid.

4. James A. Fowler, "No Independent Self: An Attempt at Clarification," Christ in You Ministries 2005; http://www.christinyou.net/pages/noindependentself .html; accessed May 8, 2017.

5. Samuel Whitefield, "God's Eternal Purpose for Man," December 14, 2014; https://samuelwhitefield.com/1519/gods-eternal-purpose-for-man; accessed May 5, 2017.

6. Norman Grubb, *The Liberating Secret* (Blowing Rock, NC: Zerubbabel Press, 2010), 114–115.

7. A group of Moravian families, fleeing bitter persecution for their faith, found refuge in 1722 in Saxony, Germany, on the estate of Count Nicholas von Zinzendorf (1700–1760), a pietist nobleman. They built the community of Herrnhut, which became a safe haven for many other persecuted Christians. The Moravians experienced a great outpouring of the Spirit in 1727 that was later called the Moravian Pentecost. They were known for Christian unity. On his deathbed, von Zinzendorf said with joy that he had seen the prayer of Jesus for unity in John 17 answered in his lifetime.

8. Gregory Mantle, *Beyond Humiliation: The Way of the Cross* (Minneapolis, MN: Bethany House Publishers, 1975), 64–65.

9. Watchman Nee, *The Normal Christian Life* (Fort Washington, PA: CLC Ministries International with permission of Tyndale House Publishers, Inc., 2009. Previously published 1957 and 1977), 9–10.

CHAPTER 16

OPENING ANCIENT WELLS

God is opening ancient spiritual wells that have not only been capped for many years but are hardly even mentioned in a great many of our churches. The most important forgotten well is the deep work of the cross available to us through the death, resurrection, and ascension of Christ. The enemy has plugged the wells of revival and awakening in the church, but God is directing His servants to reopen the wells and allow the fountain of the water of life to flow freely once again.

I will open rivers in desolate heights, and fountains in the midst of the valleys; I will make the wilderness a pool of water, and the dry land springs of water (Isaiah 41:18).

WELLS OF LIFE

Spiritual wells from the past are being rediscovered. History holds keys that unlock secrets and lead to hidden pathways. Mysteries and gates of old are being recovered by the church.

He said to them, Therefore every teacher and interpreter of the Sacred Writings who has been instructed about and trained for the kingdom of heaven and has become a disciple is like a

*householder who brings forth out of his storehouse **treasure**
that is new and [treasure that is] old [the fresh as well as
the familiar]* (Matthew 13:52 AMPC).

We are living in a time of restoration and recovery of those
things lost. The Lord will finish what He has begun. Moreover, He
has saved His best wine for last. What God initiated in the past,
He will complete with greater glory.

Isaac, the son promised to Abraham, is a unique figure in the
book of Genesis. He is a patriarch about whom little is written
compared to all that we know about his father

***God has saved His
best wine for last.***

Abraham and his son Jacob, yet he lived the lon-
gest. Almost nothing is recorded about his adult
life after his marriage to Rebekah. We only learn
that he never set foot outside the land of Israel and that he dug
wells. Most of Genesis chapter 26 is devoted to his well re-digging
efforts. At that time, it was vital to have a water supply to survive
in the arid land.

When Isaac arrived at Gerar, he discovered that the Philis-
tines, enemy of the Jews, had stopped up the wells Abraham had
once dug. Isaac reopened the wells of Abraham, his father's legacy,
and dug some new wells of his own. Isaac had both a hereditary
right and the responsibility to reopen the ancient wells. We have
an inheritance and responsibility to reopen the wells of life for our
generation as well.

*The water I give will be an artesian spring within, gushing
fountains of endless life* (John 4:14 MSG).

RESTORATION OF THE CHURCH

To see the future, look to the past. There truly is nothing
new under the sun. Everything that may have seemed strange for

those living in times of revival has already been recorded in the pages of history.

> Charismatic Christianity is not solely a twentieth century phenomenon. It has been around since Jesus walked the earth 2,000 years ago.... Is this expression of spirituality simply heresy and fanaticism, as some would charge? Is it merely a marginal expression of true Christianity, as others would suggest? Or is it, in fact, a restoration of true biblical Christianity?"[1]

We believe the answer to the final question is "yes." A dry, powerless Church is not the Church Jesus is building.

The Church was born 2,000 years ago, around A.D. 30, on the Day of Pentecost. The glory of God burst upon the scene and ordinary men and women were set ablaze with holy fire. They turned the world upside down. However, following A.D. 70, the formerly brilliant light began to grow dim. Jerusalem fell. The Jews were dispersed. The Christian religion was forbidden, followers *To see the future, look to the past.* of Christ became outlaws, and the years from A.D. 100 to A.D. 313 were marked by severe persecution. The most horrible persecution occurred during the reign of Diocletian and lasted from A.D. 303 to A.D. 310.

Barbarian hordes destroyed the ancient civilizations of Greece and Rome and swept through Europe. What was formerly called the Dark Ages was aptly named. Even the ability to read was lost by the general population. God was moving in the darkness, however, and every generation contained a few believers who kept alive the secrets of the Spirit. A remnant always kept the torch of the testimony burning. In studying the lives of the saints of old, we read of hidden streams, strange miracles, and ancient pathways.

In A.D. 313, the Emperor Constantine had a vision of the cross before battle that assured him of victory in the name of the Christian God. The time of persecution ended and the time of prosperity began. The spiritual Church faded away and the structural Church dominated until the Reformation began more than 1,200 years later.[2] Christianity became the state-sponsored church.

The Church continued her spiritual and moral deterioration until the midnight of the Dark Ages—the 200-year span of time prior to and following A.D. 1000.

Something shifted in history at that time. God began to restore what had been lost. The time of restoration that God had promised through the mouth of the apostle Peter in the book of Acts 3:19-21 started slowly, then began to accelerate:

Repent therefore and be converted, that your sins may be blotted out, so that times of refreshing may come from the presence of the Lord, and that He may send Jesus Christ, who was preached to you before, whom heaven must receive until the times of restoration of all things, which God has spoken by the mouth of all His holy prophets since the world began.

With the Renaissance, meaning "rebirth," came a revival of scholasticism. The ability to read was restored to the general population. In the 14th Century, scholars such as John Wycliffe in Great Britain and John Huss in Bohemia (now part of the Czech Republic) translated the Bible into the common languages of the people. In 1415, Huss was burned at the stake for doing so. Johannes Gutenberg invented the printing press in 1450. His first and most famous printing project was the Gutenberg Bible printed in 1452. Suddenly, the Bible became accessible to lay people.

In 1517, a monk named Martin Luther nailed a document called the "95 Theses" to the door of Wittenberg Castle church in 1517, proposing two central beliefs. First, the Bible is the central religious authority; and second, that individuals are saved by faith and not works. The remaining 93 theses supported the first two and criticized the practice of giving indulgences (selling forgiveness of sins to raise money). This became the foundation of the Protestant Reformation.

The Protestant Reformation both reinvigorated the Church and caused fierce waves of persecution to spread across the civilized world. Many believers fled to the American colonies for safety. The Pilgrims themselves were refugees from England who fled to America for religious freedom. Many of the Founders were descendants of refugees, including Paul Revere whose father was a French Huguenot. Thomas Paine wrote of America in his book *Common Sense:* "The reformation was preceded by the discovery of America, as if the Almighty graciously meant to open a sanctuary to the persecuted in future years, when home should afford neither friendship nor safety."

God is still on the move restoring truths that were lost during the deterioration of the church.[3]

THREE AWAKENINGS AND THE CROSS

Historically, most revivals are refreshings of the Spirit but don't restore a doctrinal truth back to the church. The Layman's Prayer Revival of 1857 is one example.[4] Those that do bring back a lost truth are called *movements*, such as the Protestant Movement. However, the Awakenings in America are especially significant movements because they restored the experiential work of the cross in the lives of believers.

We have an inheritance and responsibility to reopen the wells of life.

The Forgiven Life. The First Great Awakening in America during the first half of the eighteenth century proclaimed the message of forgiveness and salvation throughout the 13 colonies (the

Forgiven Life). The salvation experience broke down denominational divisions and united the colonies in a common salvation experience making America truly one nation under God for the first time.[5] The reality of salvation by the Son of God became an experience, not just doctrine.

The Replaced Life. The Second Great Awakening ushered in a holiness movement that lasted from the late eighteenth century through the middle of the nineteenth century. *"[I]t is no longer I who live, but Christ lives in me"* (Galatians 2:20). The Holy Spirit was made known to the church. In the century that followed, the gifts of the Spirit were released to the Church, including miracles of physical healing.

The Enthroned Life. It has been prophesied that the coming awakening, the Third Great Awakening, will ignite a great company of overcomers who will walk in power, authority, and glory and do *the "greater works"* about which Jesus spoke in John 14:10-12 because the Father will make Himself known to the church in a new way.

DEEP WATERS

The three levels of the cross—the Forgiven Life, the Replaced Life, and the Enthroned Life—can be likened to the levels of Ezekiel's river of life that flowed from the base of the temple (see Ezekiel 47:1-12). Ezekiel shares his vision about being led into the depths of the river of God. When we have a vision, the Holy Spirit controls it, and we only observe what He reveals to us. Likewise, to enter spiritual experience, we don't initiate. The Lord must take us into deep waters.

Ezekiel was first in ankle-deep water. Because he was at the shoreline, he could easily step back into the world while enjoying a measure of blessing. Next, Ezekiel journeyed into knee deep then waist-deep water in a deeper surrender to the Spirit. At this level, he still retained a measure of control. Ezekiel next found himself in waters too deep to touch bottom. Finally, he reached the point of complete surrender. He now only went where the mighty river flowed; It had become for him *"water in which one must swim, a river that could not be crossed"* (Ezekiel 47:5).

> The greatest obstacle to knowing God's plan for our lives is the persistence of our own unbending purposes and preferences. Dealing with that stubborn will may be the most important single factor in discerning and doing the will of God. How can we deal with it?[6]

TOTAL SURRENDER

The apostle Paul beseeches us to take the way of total surrender in Romans 12:1-2:

> *I beseech you therefore, brethren, by the mercies of God, that you present your bodies a living sacrifice, holy, acceptable to God, which is your reasonable service. And do not be conformed to this world, but be transformed by the renewing of your mind, that you may prove what is that good and acceptable and perfect will of God.*

Let's look more closely at what Paul is saying here. Chapters 9–11 of the book of Romans reveal Paul's own life at the third level of the cross—the deepest level of the river. In light of his own testimony, he pleads with believers to also take the way of total surrender as a *living sacrifice* on the altar of God (v.1). He then describes that sacrifice as one that is holy, or separated from the world and set apart only for God. Such a sacrifice is well-pleasing to God and worthy of His acceptance. In light of the price Jesus paid for us, this request is one that is quite reasonable. Jesus gave everything for us; we now have the opportunity to give our all for Him. As animal sacrifices were offered in the Old Testament under the Law, we now have the opportunity to sacrifice our lives unto God, wholly committed to serving Him and doing His will.

Therefore, we need to see things in a new light (v. 2). To avoid being conformed to the world, we must understand and accept God's perspective rather than conforming to the world's way of thinking. The Greek word for "renew" is *anakainosis*, referring to the adjustment of moral and spiritual vision so we think as God thinks. In doing so, we find ourselves transformed as our inner convictions change our outward behavior.

Paul concludes by telling us that God's will is good, acceptable, and perfect. He is not referring to three different levels of the will of God but describing three different attributes.

Good. Gk. *agathos.* God's will is good because God is good and He only wills that which is good. If anything is God's will, it contains the essence of God's goodness.

Acceptable. Gk. *euareston.* God's will is worthy of being received, or accepted. The word *acceptable* emphasizes the goodness of the will of God. Good is that which is worthy of our acceptance. Good is defined by God's will and that makes it something we should readily accept.

Perfect. Gk. *teleion. Teleion* means "fulfillment of intended purpose." The word *perfect* in the New Testament is defined in the context of love.[7] God is Perfect Love. Love desires only good for others. Therefore, God's will for us is full of His love. The words of Jesus, *"Be perfect, therefore, as your heavenly Father is perfect,"* refer to keeping the Great Commandment to love God and others just as God loves (Matthew 5:48).

[T]he command...that we do what is "good, acceptable, and perfect" throws us back again on the "mercies of God" in Christ. And this mercy sends us back again to pursue perfect obedience. No one can stand at the cross receiving mercy and be casual about the will of God. The cross impels us with great gratitude and hope and joy to cut off our hands, if we must, to follow Christ. So let us live at the cross for merciful blessing, and let us carry the cross in merciful obedience.[8]

Paul next tells us that when we forsake the world's way of thinking and our mind-set (our entire being) is transformed into a heavenly mind-set, we can *prove*, or approve, God's will. The word *prove* is the Greek word *dokimazo*. It means "to test with the expectation of approving." Much as a customs official decides what can be brought from one country into another, we become "officials at the gate" who allow the good, acceptable, and perfect things of Heaven to enter into this world. We become channels of God's glory and expressions of His goodness.

Prove the good, acceptable, and perfect will of God.

At each level of the cross, God cares for us and blesses us. At all depths of the river, we can still enjoy a portion of God's blessings and plan for our lives. We can also fail to progress and stay at any level we choose, thereby failing to claim our full inheritance. It is also possible to operate in highly developed spiritual gifts and have a successful ministry at the spiritual level of a child or young person (1 John 2:12-14). Progressing to the second and third levels requires greater surrender, deeper intimacy with the Lord, and a more radical work of the cross.

"Take up your cross, and follow Me."

NOTES

1. Eddie Hyatt, *2000 Years of Charismatic Christianity: A 21st Century Look at Church History from a Pentecostal/Charismatic Perspective*, (Lake Mary, FL: Charisma House, 2000), 1.

2. Bill Hamon, *The Eternal Church: A Prophetic Look at the Church—Her History, Restoration, and Destiny* (Shippensburg, PA: Destiny Image Publishers, Inc., revised edition, 2003. Originally published 1981), 88.

3. Ibid., 176.

4. Oliver Price, "The Layman's Prayer Revival of 1857–1858," *Pray with Christ Ministries*; http://www.praywithchrist.org/prayer/layman.php; accessed October 6, 2017.

   Jeremiah Lanphier, a concerned layman, started a noon prayer meeting for New York businessmen. Only six people came to the first prayer meeting on September 23, 1857 on the third floor of the "Consistory" of the Old Dutch Reformed Church on Fulton Street. By spring daily prayer meetings sprang up in many locations and daily attendance grew to 10,000…. It was called the Layman's Prayer Revival because laymen led it…. Hundreds of people who had always spent their nights in the gates of hell came to the prayer meetings that had begun in the evenings. Thousands forsook crime and became devoted followers of Christ. Crime and vice drastically declined. Wealthy people generously helped the poor whom they regarded as their brothers and sisters. Ships coming into New York harbor came under the power of God's presence. On one ship a captain and 30 men were converted to Christianity before the ship docked. Four sailors knelt for prayer down in the depths of the battleship North Carolina anchored in the harbor. They began to sing and their ungodly shipmates came running down to make fun, but the power of God gripped them and they humbly knelt in repentance.

5. Peter Marshall and David Manuel, *The Light and the Glory*, (Old Tappan, NJ: Fleming H. Revell Co., 1977), 166.

6. Richard Strauss, "Not My Will," *How to Really Know the Will of God*, April 19, 2005; https://bible.org/seriespage/6-not-my-will; accessed October 5, 2017.

7. William Greathouse, *Love Made Perfect: Foundations for the Holy Life*, (Kansas City, MO: Bethany Hill Press of Kansas City, 1997), 16–17.

8. John Piper, "What Is Good, Acceptable, and Perfect?" *Desiring God Ministry*, September 29, 2004; http://www.desiringgod.org/articles/what-is-good-and-acceptable-and-perfect; accessed May 17, 2017.

CHAPTER 17

THE ETERNAL PURPOSE OF GOD

Give me a hundred men who hate nothing but sin and love God with all their hearts and I will shake the world for Christ!—John Wesley

The thrilling accounts of revivals and awakenings that have stirred the hearts of men and women and transformed nations over the past two thousand years are not just encounters with God but signposts pointing to the potential of sold-out Christianity! When we become desperate enough, history shows us that God comes in His glory to dwell in our midst. That is normal "church"—the way God intended from the beginning: *"a dwelling place of God in the Spirit"* (Eph. 2:22).

> *Now to Him who is able to do exceedingly abundantly above all that we ask or think, **according to the power that works in us**, to Him be **glory in the church** by Christ Jesus to all generations, forever and ever* (Ephesians 3:20-21).

The Lord created us to *be* someone—sons and daughters restored to the glory of God. The Lord also created us to *do* something *with* Him! John Wesley says in *How to Pray*, "I continue to dream and pray about a revival of holiness in our day…in which each person can be unleashed through the empowerment of the Spirit to fulfill God's creational intentions."

The book of Ephesians unveils the eternal purpose of God from His perspective. This purpose includes a goal and a means of accomplishing it according to *"the eternal purpose which He accomplished in Christ Jesus our Lord"* (Ephesians 3:11). It reveals that God's eternal purpose is to express Himself through humanity in the body of Christ, composed of sons of God restored to the glory of God.

"We are His workmanship, created in Christ Jesus for good works, which God prepared beforehand that we should walk in them" (Ephesians 2:10). That is His will for our life. At the climax of the Song of Solomon, the Shulamite and her Bridegroom King go forth to labor together, and she discovers the joy of fellowship in purpose: *"Come, my beloved, let us go forth"* (see Song of Solomon 7:11-13). Intimacy is combined with action.

Intimacy is combined with action.

As His time on earth drew to a close, Jesus told His Father, *"I have glorified You on the earth. I have finished the work which You have given Me to do"* (John 17:4). On the cross, Jesus cried out in triumph, *"It is finished!"* (John 19:30). Likewise, God had a plan for Paul and, as he neared the end of his life, Paul proclaimed, *"I am already being poured out as a drink offering, and the time of my departure is at hand, I have fought the good fight, I have finished the race, I have kept the faith"* (2 Timothy 4:7). When Paul stood before King Agrippa, he testified, *"I was not disobedient to the heavenly vision"* (Acts 26:19). Purpose is the only way to find genuine fulfillment in life. Like Jesus and Paul, may we say, *"I delight to do Your will, O my God!"* (see Psalm 40:8; Hebrews 10:7).

> God...[created] man in order for man to be like Christ, having the life as well as the glory of Christ. As God manifests Himself through Christ, so the latter manifests Himself through man. God calls us in order that we might

become partakers of His Son, being made to be conformed to the image of His Son so that His Son might become the firstborn among many brethren. From eternity past up to the resurrection the Lord is the only begotten Son. But after He is raised from the dead He becomes the firstborn Son.... By the death of God's only begotten Son, many sons are born....

The Son came to be man, being made a little lower than the angels; but He is later on crowned with glory and honor. He is to lead many sons into glory. The reason why God creates man is that man might receive the life of His Son and enter into glory with His Son.[1]

The need Father God has is for *sons*. He sent Jesus, His Son, to us to accomplish His plan for redemption on our behalf. Now we can join Him in His ongoing work of redemption. Father God loves us all, but He longs for those who share His heart of sacrificial love for others! Jesus *"did not come to be served, but to serve, and to give His life a ransom for many"* (Matthew 20:28).

We are *predestined* to be sons of God.[2] The word *predestined* as used here means that our *purpose is preordained*, not that we will automatically comply with that purpose. We never lose our ability to choose. The Father *"chose us in Him before the foundation of the world, that we should be holy and without blame before Him in love, having predestined us to* **adoption as sons** *by Jesus Christ"* (Ephesians 1:4-5).

Father God longs for sons.

How do *sons* of God differ from *children* of God? The Greek word for "son" is *huios*, referring to one who has reached full maturity and is a worthy heir to his father's name, authority, possessions, and responsibilities: a son who is ready to take his place in his father's business.

Christian progression from spiritual children to spiritual sons means the enemy's very undoing…. [T]he traditional Hebrew view of "the adoption of a son" has absolutely nothing to do with the placement of an orphan into a foster home, rather, it has to do with a young man coming into a place of maturity whereby the full authority and resources of his father are bestowed upon him.[3]

*For the earnest expectation of the creation eagerly waits for the **revealing of the sons of God** (Romans 8:19).*

From eternity to eternity God has a plan; that is to say, He wants sons. Many Christians cannot envisage the greatness of this matter of sons. Yet we know from Scripture that God's purpose is to obtain sons…. [A]t the time when God's purpose is realized there shall be many sons in glory, for the beloved Son of God will bring many sons unto glory. God's purpose is to obtain sons, and these sons, in turn are His inheritance…. What is meant by the inheritance of God? God's inheritance means that something that belongs to Him. God has fore-ordained us saints to be His inherited possession…to be like God, to be able to glorify Him.[4]

We are predestined to be sons of God.

COUNT THE COST

Just as *"not I, but Christ"* calls us into the Replaced Life, *"present your bodies a living sacrifice"* summons us to the third level of the Cross as overcoming sons and daughters of God, or the *Enthroned Life* (see Galatians 2:20; Romans 12:1). At each great level of surrender, we must count the cost (see Luke 14:28). Admission to the Enthroned Life requires total surrender. The first two levels are for personal victory; the third level is a surrender of our body in the service of others just as Jesus allowed the Father to carry out His will in the life of His Son.

The book of Romans lays out the levels of surrender from the perspective of humankind. Romans 1-5 present the necessity and the means of salvation through forgiveness. Romans 6–7 show the way of personal victory over sin and legalistic self-effort through replacement. Romans 8 is an interim chapter that presents our freedom from condemnation and striving. It also points the way to the third level, the Enthroned Life, in which we share the throne of Jesus. Beginning in Romans 8:13, we move into a new theme—the overcoming sons of God.

*"To him who **overcomes I will grant to sit with Me on My throne**, as I also overcame and sat down with My Father on His throne"* (Revelation 3:21). The Enthroned Life is one that has entered sonship, which is the position of the overcomer. The sons of God who are restored to the glory, power, and authority of God are those

The Enthroned Life is the position of the overcomer.

who are *"led by the Spirit of God, these are sons of God"* (Romans 8:14). Being led by the Spirit is different from walking in the Spirit. The word *lead*, Greek *ago*, used here means to conduct, to lead by laying hold of and bring to the point of destination. It is the same word used in the sense of a rider on a horse, a pilot of a plane, or a guide for a blind person.

In Romans 9–11, Paul uses himself as an example of one who has passed through the narrow gate and walked the Highway of Holiness to a life surrendered for the sake of serving others (see Matthew 7:13-14; Isaiah 35:7-9). Paul says in effect, "In light of what a life of service means and what I have told you": *"I beseech you therefore, brethren, by the mercies of God, that you **present your bodies a living sacrifice**, holy, acceptable to God, which*

The Enthroned Life requires total surrender.

is your reasonable service" (Romans 12:1). Just as Jesus presented His body to be fully used by His Father during His earth walk, Paul now exhorts us to also present our body as living sacrifice to dedicate our life to accomplishing God's will.

> *Therefore, when He came into the world, He said: "Sacrifice and offering You did not desire, but **a body You have prepared for Me.** ... 'Behold, I have come...to do Your will, O God'"* (Hebrews 10:5-7).

The eternal purpose of God is centered in God Himself, not individuals...although He includes people in His plan. The book of Ephesians lays out the eternal purpose of God as no other book in the Bible. While Romans is written according to human perspective, problems, and needs, Ephesians is written from the position of the One seated together with the Father in heavenly places. When it comes to understanding this book, we need to pray:

> Lord, take me out of my condition, away from the earth, and outside of time. Lord, rescue me from my condition and bring me into eternity and into the heavenlies. I want to enter into the heart of God and into His eternal purpose.[5]

A HEAVENLY PATTERN

Our life on earth becomes significant in eternity when we passionately pursue God's eternal purpose and co-labor with Him in fulfilling His eternal plan. God is searching for such sons and daughters. We have an inheritance in Christ, but the Father has an inheritance in us! Paul prays that we will understand *"the riches of the glory"* of the Father's *"inheritance in the saints"* (Ephesians 1:18).

The Father has an inheritance in the saints.

The Lord spoke to me (Dennis) that, in the pursuit of God Himself, relationship grows only as we persevere in seeking Him. The Lord revealed a clear pattern in the development of intimacy and spiritual maturity as well as the potential for both the increasing union and the tragedy of failure to continue at any point on the journey. The *"path of the just is like the shining sun, that shines ever brighter unto the perfect day"* (Proverbs 4:18). The pattern is this:

Touch leads to embrace. Touching the presence of God is wonderful, but that is only the beginning. Some believers wander from conference to conference hoping for a touch, but the touch that counts the most is the daily encounter in our prayer closet. Every time the Lord touches us, it leaves an imprint of the divine nature on our heart. When we persevere, the gentle touch becomes a holy embrace. In this stage, we must pursue a forgiveness lifestyle to keep the channel clear both vertically with God and horizontally with people. Unforgiveness is sin, and sin creates walls. Only sin can separate us: *"[Y]our iniquities have separated you from your God; and your sins have hidden His face from you"* (Isaiah 59:2).

Unforgiveness is sin, and sin creates walls.

Embrace gives satisfaction. Touch can be intermittent. Embrace, on the other hand, leads to a satisfaction that lingers. Embrace includes longing for more. We become strong in spirit with an increasing ability to quickly resist temptation. *"His left hand is under my head, and his right hand embraces me"* (Song of Solomon 2:6). Like Abraham, God Himself rather than the applause of people becomes the only reward we desire (see Genesis 15:1).

God is the only reward we desire.

Satisfaction points to abounding love. Satisfaction leads to a bonding in spiritual union. It also includes a heart change toward other people. We become *"poor in spirit,"* or humble of heart, knowing that Christ is our life, and without Him filling our vessel

We have the eyes and heart of Jesus.

we are nothing (Matthew 5:3). We see others in light of their great need for a new spirit. *"I pray, that your love may abound still more and more in knowledge and all* [true] *discernment"* (Philippians 1:9). When we have the eyes of Jesus, we have the heart of Jesus, and His heart overflows with love and compassion.

Abounding love reflects the Father's heart. We have moved from God outside to God inside (the Replaced Life), to God

God's love overflows from us to others.

Universal, the One who loved from the beginning. Our focus shifts from God as the one who takes care of me to the God whose love ever-overflows on behalf of others.

The Father's heart brings sons to glory. We see the potential in people from God's perspective and long for them to know sonship and the way to Throne life. Because we now share the Father's heart, the focus of our heart turns outward to others. Unlike believers who saw but turned away from this high calling, we long

God's eternal purpose becomes our passion.

to become *"teachers of others"* (see Hebrews 5:12). God's eternal purpose becomes our passion, and we willingly share in the fellowship of Christ's sufferings with joy (see Philippians 3:10).

THREE ELEMENTS OF GOD'S WILL

Three elements of God's will are revealed in Ephesians 1—the *good pleasure* of God's will, the *mystery* of His will, and the *counsel* of His will (the way to accomplish His will). God's good pleasure, His heart's desire, is centered in Christ, the Body of Christ, the church, and God forming the nature of Christ Himself in overcoming sons. Before the foundation of the earth, the three Persons of the Godhead—Father, Son, and Holy Spirit—made a decision called a "counsel." This plan was made in eternity past and is focused on dispensing the wealth of God's being into sons and that Way is Christ.

The mystery of God *is* Christ. He is the mystery of God, the embodiment of God, and the fullness of the Godhead dwells in Him bodily. The means by which God the Father will accomplish His will is through Christ. As we know Christ and experience Christ's life, Christ is formed in us, and we become like Him in the world (see 1 John 4:17). The only begotten Son of God became the firstborn of many sons restored to the glory, authority, and throne of God (see Hebrews 2:10). In this way, the Body of Christ is made up of many sons, the Bride makes herself ready, and the New Jerusalem is formed.

The Father gains sons (see Hebrews 2:10).

Jesus gains a bride (see Ephesians 5:25-28).

> *Then I, John, saw the holy city, New Jerusalem, coming down out of heaven from God, prepared as* **a bride adorned for her husband** *(Revelation 21:2).*

The first aspect of God's eternal purpose is that many sons become like Christ, having both His life and His glory. The second aspect is that all things may manifest the glory of Christ in the future. To a certain extent, all creation reveals God now. *"For since the creation of the world His invisible attributes, His eternal power and divine nature, have been clearly seen, being understood through what has been made"* (Romans 1:20 NASB). Eventually, however, all created things will be summed up in Christ and manifest the full glory of God through *"the mystery of His will, according to His good pleasure which He purposed in Himself, that in the dispensation of the fullness of the times He might gather together in one all things in Christ, both which are in heaven and which are on earth—in Him"* (Ephesians 1:9-10). Eventually,

The Father gains sons. Jesus gains a bride.

all created things will be summed up in Christ and manifest the full glory of God.

THE WAY, TRUTH, AND LIFE

In John chapter 14, Jesus declared that He Himself was **the Way** to the Father! The Way is not a plan or a journey but a mutual sharing of life. The Way is union with the Living God. When we receive a replaced spirit, we are one with His Spirit. We are partakers of His resurrection and are spiritually seated with Him in the presence of His Father.

Jesus is the Way to the Father. Jesus did not raise Himself from the dead. For three days, His body was dead in the Tomb. On the third day, Father God *"raised Him from the dead and gave Him glory"* (1 Peter 1:21). When the Father raised Jesus from the dead, He raised us, too: God *"raised Him* [Jesus] *from the dead and seated Him at His right hand in the heavenly places"* (Ephesians 1:20) and *"raised us up together, and made us **sit together in the heavenly places in Christ Jesus**"* (Ephesians 2:6).

Jesus said to His Father: *"I have declared to them Your name, and will declare it, that the love with which You loved Me may be in them, and **I in them**"* (John 17:26). And: *"Anyone who loves Me will listen to My voice and obey. The Father will love him, and **We will draw close to him and make a dwelling place within him**"* (John 14:23 The Voice Bible).

When we receive Jesus as the **Way** to our heavenly Father, through His resurrection, He replaces the spirit of error in us with the Spirit of **Truth.** Death is swallowed up in His **Life.** Through His ascension, we ascend together with Him to be in the presence of the Father (see Ephesians 2:6; Revelation 3:21). *"I am the way, the truth, and the life. **No one comes to the Father except through Me**"* (John 14:6).

Jesus tells us plainly:

*I will not leave you orphans; I will come to you. A little while longer and the world will see Me no more, but you will see Me. Because I live, you will live also. At that day you will know that **I am in My Father, and you in Me, and I in you**. ...If anyone loves Me, he will keep My word; and My Father will love him, and **We will come to him and make Our home with him*** (John 14:18-20, 23).

GREATER WORKS VERSUS GIFTS

Throughout His ministry, Jesus lived in complete dependence on His Father. *"[T]he **Son can do nothing of Himself**, but what He sees the Father do; for whatever He does, the Son also does in like manner"* (John 5:19); *"**I can of Myself do nothing**. As I hear, I judge; and My judgment is righteous, because I do not seek My own will but the will of the Father who sent Me"* (John 5:30).

In John chapter 14 at the Last Supper, Jesus lays it all out for His disciples. Finally, it was time to share the secrets of Heaven with them

The Son can do nothing of Himself.

even though they wouldn't understand until later. He told them that He was making a spiritual connection so that, after the cross, He would still be with them in Spirit. *"I am the **way**"* (John 14:6).

Moreover, Jesus told them He Himself was the means that would unite them with the Father and the Spirit of Holiness. They wouldn't be left as orphans after He died—resurrection and ascension were coming. Jesus made a way for them to enter the spiritual portal leading to life in the heavenly realm and the presence of His Father! No separation, only spirit-to-Spirit union: *"I am in My Father, and you in Me, and I in you"* (John 14:20).

Jesus made it abundantly clear that He did nothing apart from His Father and that He and His Father were one. Jesus inherited a throne and He shares it with us! We are co-heirs with Christ and share with Him the glory, authority, and power of the Kingdom (see Romans 8:17).

"I am in My Father, and you in Me, and I in you." I believe Jesus is asking us, "Do you wonder about the great signs and wonders I do? I don't do them of Myself. I rely on the power of My Father within Me." *"[T]he **Father** who dwells in Me **does the works**. Believe Me that **I am in the Father and the Father in Me**, or else believe Me for the sake of the works themselves* (John 14:10-11). No separation!

> *If anyone loves Me, he will keep My word; and My Father will love him, and **WE** will come to him and make Our home with him"* (John 14:23).

I believe Jesus wants us to know, "I go to make a way to take you to My Father so you can live the same kind of life I have lived. And that life includes the power of 'greater works'!" *"Most assuredly, I say to you, he who believes in Me, the works that I do he will do also; and **greater works** than these he will do, because I go to My Father"* (John 14:12).

No separation!

FLAMES OF HOLY LOVE

The greater *works* of the Father are reserved for those who gain an entrance into the *heart* of the Father and live *"hidden with Christ in God"* (Colossians 3:3). Intimacy with the Lord is the prerequisite to operate in the greater works.

> Here is the sum of the perfect law [of love], the circumcision of the heart. Let the spirit return to God that gave it, with the whole train of the affections. Other sacrifices from us He would not [desire]: but the living sacrifice of

the heart hath He chosen. Let it be continually offered up
to God, through Christ, in flames of holy love.[6]

What about spiritual gifts? Spiritual gifts are available for believers at any level. Even new believers can receive gifts of prophecy,
healing, word of knowledge, and so forth. Leaders and others who
are living in sin may continue to operate in their gifts because *"the
gifts and callings of God are irrevocable"* (Romans 11:29).

Gifts do not necessarily require close intimacy with the Lord. We would do well to
heed the words of Jesus on the matter:

***Let your heart be
offered up to God in
flames of holy love.***

*Many will say to Me in that day, "Lord, Lord, have we not
prophesied in Your name, cast out demons in Your name, and
done many wonders in Your name?" And then I will declare
to them, "I never knew you; depart from Me, you who practice lawlessness!"* (Matthew 7:22-23).

Dr. Bill Hamon writes that the prerequisite for participation
in the coming move of God is agape love:

The King James Version uses the word *charity* to denote
the "agape love" that is the very essence and nature and
character of Christ (see 1 Cor. 13:4-8 KJV). Paul knew
by revelation that the Church would never reach full maturity until fullness of love was obtained. Therefore, he
told the Church, "I pray that you, being rooted and established in love, may have power, together with all the
saints, to grasp how wide and long and high and deep is
the love of Christ, and to know this love that surpasses
knowledge—that you may be filled to the measure of all
the fullness of God" (Eph. 3:17-19 NIV).

The ultimate criterion and determining factor for those who will be participants in the next restorational move of God is whether the love character of Christ has become the inner motivating force of their lives. Present-truth Christians should not base future participation on present-day manifestations…. Spiritual manifestations or good works will not open the door, but those who have the love character of Christ will have an open door set before them that no man can shut.[7]

ROYAL PRIESTHOOD

The summit of Christian living is to be a king and priest unto God—having God's love, revealing God's glory, and exercising God's authority and power: *[Y]ou are a chosen generation, a **royal priesthood**, a holy nation, His own special people, that you may proclaim the praises of Him who called you out of darkness into His marvelous light* (1 Peter 2:9).

We are a chosen generation, a royal priesthood.

Kings. The life of Jesus reveals the kind of kings we are called to be as we *"reign as kings in life"* (Romans 5:17 AMPC). Our model King came as One who serves His people, not as a tyrant or plunderer of His peoples' goods. This kingship restores what has been stolen to the rightful owner. Jesus called His disciples to Himself and said:

> *"You know that the rulers of the Gentiles lord it over them, and those who are great exercise authority over them. Yet it shall not be so among you; but whoever desires to become great among you, let him be your servant. And whoever desires to be first among you, let him be your slave—just as **the Son of Man did not come to be served, but to serve, and to give His life a ransom for many**"* (Matthew 25-28).

As presented in the book of Ephesians, we see the progression from the Forgiven Life, to a Replaced Life for our renewal, to sharing our Lord's authority in an Enthroned Life. We are now *kings*, representatives of God's throne in the power of the Spirit to bring the captives of the devil back to the Father just as we were led back to Him ourselves.

Priests. A priest is commissioned to fulfill a saving purpose for others. We were once thirsting ones who drank. Now, others may be filled from our fullness. As priests, we stand with Christ under the order of Melchizedek, our eternal high priest, to stand in the gap between God and humankind for the sake of others.

RIVER FROM THE THRONE

Christ within is the Source of living waters springing up in our heart, the true Vine from which we draw life, the Treasure hidden in our earthen vessel, and the Doer of God's righteous will. Righteousness is God's love in action. Therefore, only Christ living within us and working through us can satisfy the righteous requirements of God.

In our union with Christ, He becomes the One who operates *as* us. As we yield to Him, He works through us. *"I delight to do Your will, O my God, and Your law is within my heart"* (Psalm 40:8). In Christ we become conduits of God's will on earth and release the living waters of the Spirit to a world lost in pain and darkness.

Christ* as *us!

> [H]e showed me **a pure river of water of life**, clear as crystal, **proceeding from the throne** of God and of the Lamb (Revelation 22:1).

NOTES

1. Watchman Nee, *God's Plan and the Overcomers* (Richmond, VA: Christian Fellowship Publishers, Inc., 1977), 12.

2. Men are included in the Bride of Christ and women are called to be sons of God. The term *bride* refers to intimacy, and *son* denotes working with God in His eternal purpose.

3. David Weber, "The Adoption of Sons," *Sons to Glory;* http://www.sonstoglory .com/spiritualadoption.htm; accessed June 2, 2017.

4. Watchman Nee, *The Spirit of Wisdom and Revelation,* 11–12.

5. Witness Lee, *Life-Study of Ephesians* (Anaheim, CA: Living Stream Ministry, 1984), 9.

6. John Wesley, *A Plain Account of Christian Perfection* (North Charleston, SC: CreateSpace Independent Publishing Platform, 2017), 7.

7. Bill Hamon, *The Eternal Church: A Prophetic Look at the Church—Her History, Restoration, and Destiny* (Shippensburg, PA: Destiny Image Publishers, Inc., revised edition, 2003. Originally published 1981), 313–314.

ABOUT THE AUTHORS

Drs. Dennis and Jennifer Clark minister together as a husband and wife team, pastoring Kingdom Life Church in Fort Mill, South Carolina. They are also founders/directors of Full Stature Ministries. Dennis holds a Ph.D. in theology and Jennifer holds a Th.D. in theology as well as B.S., M.S., and Ed.S. degrees in psychology. Visit the authors online at www.forgive123.com.

FREE E-BOOKS?
YES, PLEASE!

Get **FREE** and deeply discounted **Christian books** for your **e-reader** delivered to your inbox **every week!**

IT'S SIMPLE!

VISIT lovetoreadclub.com

SUBSCRIBE by entering your email address

RECEIVE free and discounted e-book offers and inspiring articles delivered to your inbox every week!

Unsubscribe at any time.

SUBSCRIBE NOW!

LOVE TO READ CLUB

visit **LOVETOREADCLUB.COM** ▶